teach®
yourself

backgammon

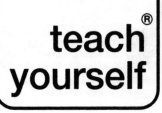

backgammon
michael crane

For UK order enquiries: please contact Bookpoint Ltd, 130 Milton Park, Abingdon, Oxon, OX14 4SB. Telephone: +44 (0) 1235 827720. Fax: +44 (0) 1235 400454. Lines are open 09.00–17.00, Monday to Saturday, with a 24-hour message answering service. Details about our titles and how to order are available at www.teachyourself.co.uk

For USA order enquiries: please contact McGraw-Hill Customer Services, PO Box 545, Blacklick, OH 43004-0545, USA. Telephone: 1-800-722-4726. Fax: 1-614-755-5645.

For Canada order enquiries: please contact McGraw-Hill Ryerson Ltd, 300 Water St, Whitby, Ontario, L1N 9B6, Canada. Telephone: 905 430 5000. Fax: 905 430 5020.

Long renowned as the authoritative source for self-guided learning – with more than 50 million copies sold worldwide – the **teach yourself** series includes over 500 titles in the fields of languages, crafts, hobbies, business, computing and education.

British Library Cataloguing in Publication Data: a catalogue record for this title is available from the British Library.

Library of Congress Catalog Card Number: on file.

First published in UK 2006 by Hodder Education, 338 Euston Road, London, NW1 3BH.

First published in US 2006 by The McGraw-Hill Companies, Inc.

This edition published 2006.

The **teach yourself** name is a registered trade mark of Hodder Headline.

Typeset by Servis Filmsetting Ltd, Manchester.
Printed in Great Britain for Hodder Education, a division of Hodder Headline, an Hachette Livre UK Company, 338 Euston Road, London, NW1 3BH, by Cox & Wyman Ltd, Reading, Berkshire.

The publisher has used its best endeavours to ensure that the URLs for external websites referred to in this book are correct and active at the time of going to press. However, the publisher and the author have no responsibility for the websites and can make no guarantee that a site will remain live or that the content will remain relevant, decent or appropriate.

Hodder Headline's policy is to use papers that are natural, renewable and recyclable products and made from wood grown in sustainable forests. The logging and manufacturing processes are expected to conform to the environmental regulations of the country of origin.

Impression number   11 10 9 8 7 6 5 4 3 2

Year   2010 2009 2008 2007

contents

I would like to dedicate this book to my dear friend, David Naylor, who is recovering from a cycling accident that occurred in the Italian Alps in 2004. May he fully recover so that he can once again start creating the most beautiful backgammon boards in the world.

acknowledgements

This book would have been impossible to write without the help and support of several people. I would like to thank the following:

- **Robin Clay**, for his first book, *Teach Yourself Backgammon* (1977), which I read and digested to get me started in playing backgammon; also for his personal assistance in improving my game.
- **Jeff Ellis, Peter Chan and Rosey Bensley** for allowing me to reproduce some of their games in order to illustrate what happens during a good game of backgammon.
- **Jake Jacobs, Michael Strato, Tom Keith and Mel Liefer** for the backgammon Internet resources that I and many others dip into on a regular basis to keep on top of this fascinating game.
- **Hercules – Baron of Culcreuch, Bill Davis, Carol Joy Cole and Chiva K. Tafazzoli** for their support in my role as an international tournament director.
- Finally, my wife, **Sharen Crane**, without whom none of this could have happened. Without her financial and moral support I would not have been able to take the step into full-time backgammon, thus allowing me to pursue my ambition to write a book such as this.

01

what is backgammon?

In this chapter you will learn:

- some general information about backgammon
- how backgammon compares with and resembles other games.

This book is for the absolute beginner; someone who's got a backgammon board at home but has never fully understood the Taiwanese English instructions that came with the set, and has therefore confined it to the cupboard under the stairs, filed away under, 'I'll learn it later.' Later has now arrived.

Even if you have already made a start at learning backgammon, I am certain there's a lot in this book you won't know. I have met backgammon players who have been 'playing' for years who haven't the first idea of how many dice rolls contain a 3, or how many combinations of rolls there are using two dice. Although it isn't absolutely necessary to know such things to enjoy a game of backgammon, it will improve your chances of winning a game.

Backgammon is a board game of fun and excitement; a game that can be enjoyed by all members of the family. There's no other game I know that is anywhere near as exciting as backgammon. Its very nature of unknown, random dice rolls guarantees that players can rarely keep quiet during a game – shouts of delight and despair are common as the game unfolds and fortunes alternate.

Backgammon is a combination of games, most of which many players have tried before turning to backgammon.

- It is a race game like ludo in that the first player to get all his checkers around the board and off is the winner.
- It is a strategy game like chess because it isn't just a simple race around the board but an absorbing tactical manoeuvre of 'armies' embroiled in an exciting battle for domination and victory, during which you have to have alternative plans as present ones fall apart on the roll of a die.
- It is a board game similar to draughts inasmuch as the checkers are the same shape and move in opposing directions in their attempt to get 'home'.

This unique combination makes backgammon a game for everyone to enjoy. A lot of the excitement in backgammon is derived from its use of dice to determine how far each checker can move; and the fun part starts when those dice rolls turn the game upside down and turn a loser into a winner. There's no better feeling than that of coming out on top when all looked lost.

Moving the checkers around the board is just a part of the game, *where* you move them and *why* you move them is vital to winning.

- In chess, moves are predictable – many of the pieces are unable to move until pieces in front of them allow them to do so.

In backgammon, all pieces can move from the outset, requiring only a roll of the dice to launch them on their way.

- In ludo, you have four checkers to take around the board and get home. In backgammon you have 15 each to get around safely; and none of them can leave the board until all of them are 'home'.
- In draughts, opposing sides fight until the last of the opponent's checkers have been taken. In backgammon you simply have to get all your checkers off first; and more points are gained if your opponent hasn't taken any of his checkers off the board.

In chess and draughts games can end in a draw or stalemate. In backgammon there's always a winner, and it is hoped that this book will ensure it is you more often than not! We all like to win and I am going to help you do it.

To sum up, backgammon is an exciting game of tactics, probabilities, strategy and chance. A game where, despite the vagaries of the dice, the more experienced and knowledgeable player will prevail in the long run. However, due to the element of chance or luck, absolute beginners can triumph over a champion – this is the appeal and fun of backgammon. Its outcome is often uncertain until the very last rolls of the game, when it can all fall apart on the roll of the dice. Backgammon is fun!

Before you go a page further, have you got a backgammon board? You'll need one to follow the positions and instructions within this book.

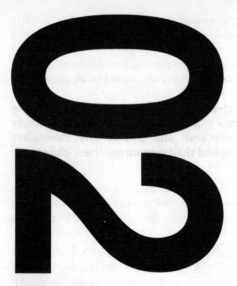

02 starting at the end!

In this chapter you will learn:

- how to end/win a game of backgammon
- that before you start a game it's important to know exactly what the aim is and how it is achieved
- that winning the game gets more complicated when an opponent threatens to hit one of your checkers and forces you to restart from the beginning
- that even greater complications arise when an opponent's checkers embed themselves in your home board during the bear-off
- how to bring your checkers home safely while an opponent tries to hit you back.

If I start at the beginning you won't have the faintest idea of what you're trying to achieve during a game of backgammon. It is much easier to explain how the game ends first – this way, when you start to play you'll know from the beginning exactly what is required to win, and how easy it can be to lose! In backgammon there can be a very fine line between winning and losing (just how fine will become clearer as you read this book). Many players lose a game from a winning position because they know little about how the game ends and how to give themselves better chances of winning and their opponents fewer chances to beat them.

We all play games to win, but if we don't know how to win when we get to the end of the game then we often end up losing – and the more you lose the sooner you'll get tired of playing. So, to win a game of backgammon you have to learn how not to lose! Too few players ever really learn how the game ends; they are too intent on getting started, and in doing so gloss over the whole point of the game – how to win.

Although we start at the end, I'll just show you the initial set-up for the start of a game and the names of the segments on the board so that you can familiarize yourself with the components.

Backgammon *boards* don't have a 'direction' of play. The direction of play is always clockwise for one player and anticlockwise for his opponent. In figure 2.1, Black (the reader), is playing anticlockwise (and is in all the board diagrams). However, if the board is viewed from white's perspective, black would be playing clockwise. Direction of play is a matter of choice, decided between the players.

The winner in backgammon, as in ludo, is the first person to get all his checkers (sometimes referred to as stones or men) around the board and off, i.e. it is a racing game. Look at figure 2.1, which shows your checkers in your home board (sometimes called the inner board). You are black and you are moving your checkers anticlockwise – from the 24-point towards your 1-point (each triangular segment is called a point). For the moment, ignore the rest of the board and concentrate on your home board. It is here that all 15 checkers have to be before you can begin the end of the game and win it.

In backgammon we use two dice and the checkers are moved, according to the numbers thrown on each of the dice, around the board from the 24-point in descending order towards the

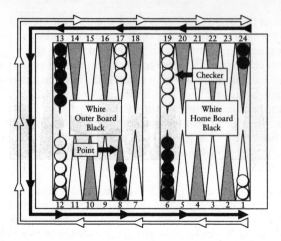

Figure 2.1

1-point. For example, if you roll 3–2, this is not a 5 but one move of 3 and then one move of 2, or one move of 2 and then one move of 3 (you can move two checkers or one checker). The order in which you move a dice roll will vary depending upon which order will benefit you most – more on this subject later. In backgammon, if you roll a doublet or double (e.g. 3–3, 5–5 etc.) you can make four moves instead of the normal two. The dice are never added together in backgammon; they remain separate but they can be used in sequence to make a greater number.

Bearing off – the end of the game

Set up your backgammon board as shown in figure 2.2. You (black) have moved all your checkers around the board from the white home board to your home board. You are now about to start 'bearing off', i.e. taking your checkers off the board at the very end of the game. Each checker bears off according to the dice roll, and this is how you win the game – by taking off all your checkers before your opponent takes his off. If you roll 3–2 you can remove one checker from the 3-point and one checker from the 2-point. If you roll a die higher than the highest point occupied, checkers can be removed from that highest point, i.e. if your highest occupied point is your 4-point and you roll 6–2, you can remove a checker from your 4-point (using the 6) and a checker from your 2-point. Doubles allow

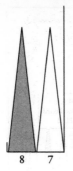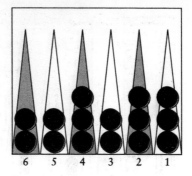

8 7 6 5 4 3 2 1

Figure 2.2

you to remove four checkers if you have enough checkers on the relevant points.

If you roll a die for a point that isn't occupied then you must, if possible, move within your home board until a die is thrown that is equal to an occupied point or a point greater than your highest occupied point. If only one die can be moved, then the higher is moved if possible, otherwise the lower one is moved. You cannot move one die then claim that the other is impossible to play – if both dice can be moved legally then you must move both of them. When referring to 'moving the die/dice', it should be remembered that it is the checkers that are moved, not the dice themselves. Throughout the book, moving any die refers to a checker that can be moved the value of the die.

Exercises

1 This first exercise is a simple one where all you have to do is bear off your checkers as efficiently as possible. Set up your home board as shown in figure 2.2 and move the following dice rolls, bearing off a checker each time: 6–1; 3–2; 4–2; 6–2.

Your board now looks like the home board segment shown in figure 2.3.

You now roll 6–2 again: take a checker off your 5-point (using the 6) and then, because you don't have any checkers on your 2-point, you now have to move within your home board. When bearing off in backgammon you want to make certain that you get as many checkers off the board as possible at each roll, and to this end the 2 is moved from the 4-point to the empty 2-point ensuring that on your next roll you will remove at least two

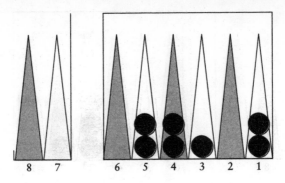

Figure 2.3

checkers. This tactic is very important when bearing off without the possibility of being hit by an opponent (more on this subject later) and is used in the next exercise. Always try to maximize the checkers you can take off on the next roll by filling empty points. Rolling dice that correspond to gaps in your home board can lose you the game, so it is vital that you concentrate on covering as many empty points as you can – preferably the lower ones.

2 Set up as in shown in figure 2.4 and move the following dice rolls, filling empty points when you can't bear-off: 2–2; 6–4; 1–1.

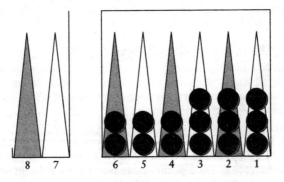

Figure 2.4

Your board should now look like figure 2.4a if you've applied the tactic of covering empty points correctly. If it doesn't look like this, have another go.

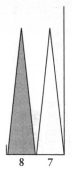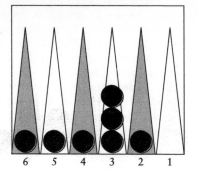

Figure 2.4a

Now reset your board to figure 2.4 again and practise on your own until you are happy with the bearing-off element of backgammon. Keep setting up and rolling until you are confident with your bearing off. There's nothing to gain by skimping this important part of the game; if you fail to bear off correctly or efficiently you may well lose the game. When you are fully satisfied with your progress we'll tackle the problem of bearing off when your opponent has checkers that can hit you and force you back to the beginning – situations that can turn a winning game into a losing game; not always because of 'lucky' dice rolls from your opponent, but often because of lack of knowledge on your part.

Bearing off against opposition on the bar

Whenever a checker is hit in backgammon, just like in ludo it has to go back to the start. A checker is hit by an opponent landing upon the same point occupied by a single checker of the opposing side; single checkers are called blots and are very vulnerable to being hit. Blots are protected by having two or more checkers of the same colour on a point – this point now belongs to that player and cannot be landed on by the opponent (although, if dice rolls allow, they can be leapt over provided that both dice rolls are not blocked). As you might have gathered, having a blot hit while you are bearing off is a major setback and is to be avoided if at all possible. Thinking ahead can reduce the risk of getting into positions in which this can occur.

The 'start' for blots that are hit is the bar, or 25-point as it is sometimes referred to (the bar is the central divider between the two halves of the board). The checker on the bar can only re-enter your opponent's home board by rolling dice that correspond to the point numbers in his home board (1 to 6, which are in fact points 24 down to 19 for the player on the bar) which are either unoccupied or are occupied by a blot or one or more of his own checkers. Points 'covered' by your opponent (two or more checkers on a single point) cannot be used to re-enter.

If any blot, anywhere on the board, is hit it will have to restart, not just the ones you might leave in your home board when bearing off against an opponent's checker on the bar (or an opponent's checkers occupying one or more of your home points after he has re-entered from the bar). Also, none of your other checkers on the board can be moved anywhere until all checkers on the bar have re-entered. The longer you spend on the bar the more moves your opponent can make without you being able to stop him. If you have two checkers on the bar and your dice roll only allows one of them to re-enter, then the remaining die is forfeit.

Blots in your home board are in great danger against opposition and must be avoided wherever possible. In figure 2.3 you have a blot on your 3-point and in figure 2.4a you have several blots! Many games that should have been won are lost when a blot is hit during the bear-off. It is hoped that this section will teach you how to avoid this.

Exercises

3 Set up as shown in figure 2.5, with an opponent on the bar, his 25-point. Now bear off, using the same dice rolls as you did in exercise 1: 6–1; 3–2; 4–2; 6–2.

   This clearly shows that if we make the same move with the 6–1, 6 off (shown as 6/0), 1/0 we leave a blot on the 6-point. If white rolls a 6 (it must be a 6 not 4–2, 5–1, 3–3 or 2–2 as these are blocked – remember, dice rolls are not added together, they are separate) on his turn he will hit your blot on re-entering and force it to restart from the bar in his home board. Remember also that while there is a checker on the bar, you cannot move any other piece until it has re-entered.

   If you are on the bar and cannot re-enter then no other checkers can be moved and your move is forfeit. This is often called **dancing** or **fanning**, and if you have any blots exposed it is likely that your opponent can hit these too! So, we play 6/0

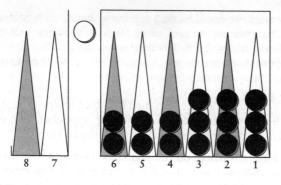

Figure 2.5

and 6/5 (6-point to 5-point) to keep the blot safe. With this in mind (assuming that white never re-enters on his roll except when there's a blot to hit), play the remaining rolls as safely as you can, bearing off when you can and moving down when you can't. Once you have completed your moves (3–2, 4–2, 6–2, and finally another 6–2) your home board should look like that shown in figure 2.5a. If your board doesn't match figure 2.5a, restart and try again. Remember, move off or down without leaving a lone checker, a blot that white could hit from the bar.

Now, it is getting quite difficult to take checkers off without leaving a blot. Do you know how many rolls leave a blot next time? Don't forget that you are using two dice so each roll is in fact two rolls! To explain: imagine you are using two different-coloured dice, one black, one white and you roll a 3–2. Either

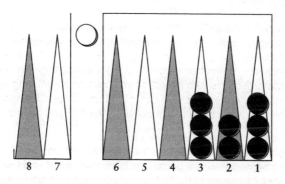

Figure 2.5a

the black die could be on 3 and the white die on 2, or it could be the other way around, white die on 3, black die on 2, but it is still only one move, 3–2. In fact, using two dice there are 36 combinations of dice rolls, so plenty to choose from! Later on you'll have a chance to learn all 36.

Back to the position in figure 2.5a. How many of those 36 possible rolls will force a blot? Don't cheat by looking at the correct answer, write them all down. You should have 25 rolls that leave a blot. A quicker way to do it is to calculate the number of rolls that don't leave a blot – there are eleven of these: 6–1, 5–1, 4–1, 3–1, 2–1, 1–1 (note that I have only shown six rolls, because non-doubles such as 6–1 and 1–6 are shown just once as 6–1 but are counted twice).

4 Practise a few bear-offs with a checker on the bar, setting up as shown in figure 2.5, and see if you can avoid leaving blots using your own dice rolls. It's not always possible to do so, but often, with a little forethought, you can considerably reduce the chances of leaving blots. This expertise is essential in playing winning backgammon and it is well worth the time taken to master it. Don't forget that you don't have to take a checker off each time. You can move within your home board if it's possible to do so, as long as you move the entire dice roll.

Also, remember that you can move either die first. Imagine that you had one checker on your 4-point and two each on the 3-, 2- and 1-points. If you rolled 6–1 in this position, to avoid leaving a blot on your 3-point, you move 4/3 with the 1, and then take off 3/0 with the 6. Perfectly legal. It is fine to move either die first, and often, the order in which you move them can make a big difference. Sometimes beginners forget they can do this and leave a blot – cheering up their opponents who are just waiting for a blot to appear to turn the game around with a timely hit.

One tip is to try to keep your top two points (the two points furthest from your 1-point) evenly distributed, looking for the bad rolls next time. As a general guide, if you are able to take 6–6 or 6–5 on the next roll without leaving a blot then you are almost 99 per cent certain not to leave a blot on the forthcoming roll no matter what it might be (note, not 100 per cent because on rare occasions blots can be left and you can do nothing about it).

Once you've mastered the tactic of bearing off safely against opposition from the bar we'll move on to opposition within your home board. This is quite likely to happen and it is very important that you fully understand how to minimize your losing chances when your opponent is waiting to hit you back on to the bar from an occupied point within your own home board.

Bearing off against opposition in your home board

Set up your home board as shown in figure 2.6. with white holding your 1-point with three checkers, and assume that white will hit any blots you expose. Now, using the same numbers as before (6–1, 3–2, 4–2, 6–2, 6–2), bear off or down safely to arrive at the position shown in figure 2.6a.

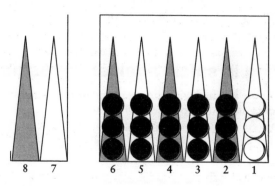

Figure 2.6

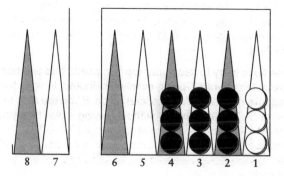

Figure 2.6a

This is a bit more difficult to arrive at. If you didn't arrive at this position, here are the rolls and moves that will achieve it:

- 6–1: 6/0 5/4
- 3–2: 3/0 2/0
- 4–2: 4/0 4/2
- 6–2: 6/0 6/4
- 6–2: 5/0 5/3.

If you calculate how many rolls will leave a blot next time, the answer is six (6–5, 6–4, 5–4).

Practise bearing off with white occupying two or more points or with a combination of checkers on points or blots and on the bar; in fact, any combination you can think of and keep doing this until you are happy with your bearing off against opposition. This knowledge is paramount in winning games in which you are leading; without it you will lose them even from such a strong racing lead. Move on to the next section only when you are ready.

Bearing in safely against opposition

We have now finished with the true 'end' of the game, so we will step back a little to a position where we approach the end of the game. As you can see, figure 2.7, showing the board at the start of the game, is divided into four segments with points num-

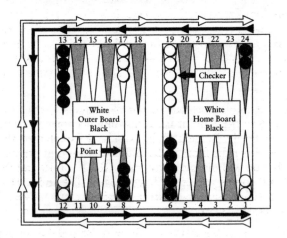

Figure 2.7

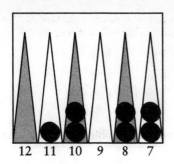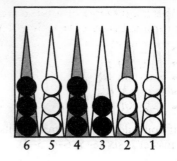

12 11 10 9 8 7   6 5 4 3 2 1

Figure 2.8

bered 1 to 24, where 24 to 19 are in your opponent's home board and points 6 to 1 are in your home board. The two remaining segments (points 18 to 7) are the outer boards; points 12 to 7 being your outer board and 18 to 13 being your opponent's outer board.

Like in draughts, checkers are moved around the board in opposing directions; in backgammon one player moves clockwise and the other anticlockwise (you, playing as black, are moving anticlockwise). Before we get to the entire board and the opening positions, let's deal with bringing checkers into your home board from your outer board. Set up as shown in figure 2.8.

Using the same rolls as before (6–1, 3–2, 4–2, 6–2), bear in (bring your checkers into your home board) safely. Straight away it is obvious that if you play the 6 by playing 10/4 (10-point to 4-point) and the 1 by playing 7/6 it will leave two blots that white can hit – so that's the wrong move! Remember, if a blot is hit it has to re-enter off the bar into the opponent's home board – a long way from home.

The correct move is to play from the 11-point, but you can't move the 6 to the 5-point because white occupies it, so how do you do it? Easily. Remember in exercise 4 I explained that you can move either die first? Well, in this case (and in others which no doubt you will discover) you move the 1, 11/10 and then the 6, 10/4. Of course you could have moved 10/4 and 11/10, but I am trying to encourage you to think about your moves. So, we play 6–1 as 11/10, 10/4.

Now for the 3–2. We can't play 3s or 2s from the 8- or 7-points without leaving a blot, so we move two checkers down from the

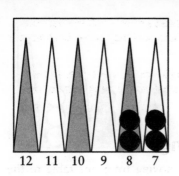
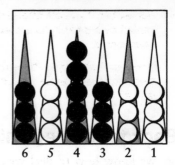

| 12 | 11 | 10 | 9 | 8 | 7 | | 6 | 5 | 4 | 3 | 2 | 1 |

Figure 2.8a

10-point, 10/7, 10/8, keeping it all nice and safe. White will only win this game if he hits a blot – and the last thing you want to do is hand the game to him by leaving one. Many winning positions are turned into losing ones by leaving unforced blots.

Now, 4–2; remember that we need to keep (if possible) an even number of checkers on our top two points and in order to achieve this we need to move one checker from the 8-point and another from the 7-point thus: 8/6, 7/3. Now, when you roll the 6–2 it is evident that you cannot move a 6 because white is blocking you by holding your 2- and 1-points, so all you can move is a 2. You don't want to leave a blot at all, so the only 2 you can move safely is 6/4, leaving you in the position show in figure 2.8a.

Exercise

5   Although the position in figure 2.8a might be a little contrived, this sort of position can occur. From this position, roll your own dice and bear in and off as safely as you can. When you have finished, set up the position shown in figure 2.8 as often as necessary and practise until you are confident with bearing in and off against opposition. Once you have gained confidence you could also place a white checker on the bar, or change the points occupied by white. Try to keep to a minimum any blots you have to leave. Look to the next roll each time and try to predict, using your knowledge of the 36 dice combinations, which is the safer play each time.

Always bear in mind that even though you might think you're winning the game, getting hit during the bear-off can reverse the situation in just one dice roll. The first player to get *all* his checkers off is the winner, not the first to get *one* checker off!

Remember, if you are hit and have to re-enter off the bar you cannot bear off any more checkers until they are all back in your home board.

When you're happy with bearing in and off we'll start at the beginning of the game. This is what you've been waiting for, isn't it?

Back to the beginning

So, we know how to deal with moving from one **table** to the other and how to avoid leaving blots wherever possible. Now let's look at the beginning of the game.

Refer to the starting position shown in figure 2.7 and set up your own board in the same way. Turn the board around to view the starting position for white (to see the starting position for a player playing in a clockwise direction). You are moving all your checkers around the board into your home board and then bearing them all off to win – simple! The problem is, white is doing the same – and you have to stop him. You stop white achieving this by blocking his moves by constructing **primes** (two or more points in a row occupied by two or more of your own checkers). These primes are used to contain your opponent's checkers and to restrict their movement around the board – but, as you've guessed, he is doing the same! It is this tactical blocking and escaping that makes backgammon so exciting.

You know what a blot is and that it is desirable not to leave any, so the best way around the board is by making points and, if possible, joining those points into primes (two or more consecutive points owned by a player). To 'make a point', all you need are two or more of your checkers on the same point. If you look at the board in figure 2.7 you'll see that you already start with four points each.

Now that you have all this background knowledge, in Chapter 3 we'll look at the standard opening moves.

03 the opening moves

In this chapter you will learn:

- which rolls work for you rather than against you
- how to make points with your first roll
- about using checkers to make points using future rolls
- how to escape a back checker in preparation for the race
- what an opponent's opening roll might be.

All backgammon sets should include four dice. For tournament play, to begin a game of backgammon each player picks his dice thus: your opponent takes one, you take one, they take another and you take the final one. Of course, for a friendly game between family members or friends, this sequence isn't too important.

To start, each player rolls one die into the right-hand side of the board (never into the table on your left-hand side – more on why not later) and, as long as the die lies flat upon the playing surface (not on top of any checkers or leaning at an angle against a checker or the side of the board – referred to as 'cocked'), the player rolling the higher die uses both dice as his opening roll. If both players roll the same number (6–6, 5–5 or any double) then both players roll again; this means that you never start the game with a double (although the second move – your opponent's first – can be a double). It is quite important that the dice roll is totally random and rolls that are not shaken well or thrown from a discernible height could be deemed invalid during a tournament – although this is not crucial in friendly games it is a good habit to get into. After this first roll, each player then continues in turn to roll both his dice.

Moving checkers in backgammon isn't as strict as in chess, where the 'touch move' is in play (in chess, once a piece is touched or moved, it has to be played; the player cannot change his mind and move a different piece). You are allowed to move any checkers you want, back and forth until you are satisfied with their final position. You then indicate the end of your turn by picking up both dice. During your turn your opponent isn't allowed to touch or interfere with any checkers (including his own). When you have completed your turn, your opponent then shakes and rolls his dice and thus the game continues. If, during your move, you make an illegal move, perhaps placing a checker on the wrong point, then your opponent has the choice of leaving the checker where it is or making you replay it correctly before he roll his own dice.

If a checker is hit during a move then it must be placed on the bar ready for re-entry. Any checkers removed in the bear-off must be removed totally from the playing surface – this is very important in tournaments; if you accidentally place a borne-off checker on the bar instead of off the board and you pick up your dice to conclude your move, the checker on the bar will remain there at your opponent's discretion and will have to re-enter and go around the board back to your home board before being borne off again.

Opening moves are in three categories: **point makers, builders** and **runners**. The annotation used (8/5, 6/5) refers to moving one checker from the 8-point to the 5-point and one checker from the 6-point to the 5-point. If you are unsure where on the board these points are, use a strip of paper to number all the points on your board as shown in figure 2.7.

Point makers

As the name implies, these rolls accomplish the very thing you set out to do, make points. A point is made by placing two of your own checkers on a single point or triangle. Making points in backgammon is key to stopping your opponent from getting around the board before you do. They form blocks or primes that stop or inhibit your opponent's movement and they act as safe havens for your own checkers on their journey around the board. Blocks or primes are where two or more made points are grouped together in such a way that an opponent cannot land upon those points. Point-making rolls are shown in the table below in order of preference.

Point makers		
Roll	Move	
3–1	8/5 6/5	a
6–1	13/7 8/7	b
4–2	8/4 6/4	c
5–3	8/3 6/3	d
6–4	8/2 6/2	e

a) This is the best point to hold (the 20-point, called the **golden point**) in either table. This is known, when it occupies an opponent's 5-point (your 20-point) as an **advanced anchor**. An **anchor** is a point held by an opponent in your home board; an advanced anchor is one where the back checkers have moved from the 24-point to the 21- or 20-points. They offer safe landings for blots (checkers that have been hit) re-entering off the bar. Occupying your 5-point is very important – it stops your opponent making it and obtaining a safe landing spot for his own checkers coming in off the bar.

b) The **bar-point** (7-point) blocks your opponent's 6s and makes it difficult to escape the back checkers (also known as runners). Also, these can become part of a prime later.

c) This move makes an important home point and a block for 4s off the bar.

d) This move is perhaps a little too deep. It's better to keep points closer together and in descending order from the 6-point if possible, but nonetheless, worth making.

e) Probably too deep for a point for advanced players, this move is acceptable for a beginner (see 6–4 in the Runner table). However, new thinking among backgammon players (brought about by software programs that play the game to a very high standard – more on these later) is that making the 2-point isn't as weak as first thought.

Builders

Although single checkers are blots, they are also builders for points (as is any spare checker on a point, or points themselves in many cases). Builders are very important and are used to make points and construct primes, and to hit an opponent's blot if the occasion arises is often desirable. Building rolls are in two categories shown as a and b in the table below.

Builders		
Roll	Move	
5–4	13/8 13/9	a
4–3	13/9 13/10	a
5–2	13/8 13/11	a
3–2	13/10 13/11	a
2–1	13/11 24/23	b
4–1	13/9 24/23	b
5–1	13/8 24/23	b

a) These moves are **mid-point builders** (13-point) and are only vulnerable to an indirect hit (i.e. the roll of two dice is required to hit, e.g. anything greater than a 6). Although these blots might be hit, the benefits are worth the risk – and backgammon is about taking calculated risks. Imagine you left a blot only six points away (a direct shot) from an opponent's checker; it will be hit 17 rolls out of 36, but if you leave an indirect shot of say seven or eight points away, then only six out of 36 (maximum shots for an indirect shot) will hit. So, when considering leaving a blot/builder, remember to keep well away from your opponent's checkers. Many beginners fail to see the potential of builders and often, when rolling 5–2, 4–3, 3–2 or 4–1 play them as a 7 or a 5 and move from their 13-point to 'safety' on their 6-point or 8-point. This is wrong and a complete waste of a roll.

b) These are splitting builders, or **minor splits** as they are known, creating builders for the outer/home board and starting off a runner (back checker), which can threaten your opponent's tables with a possible direct or indirect shot. A minor split is when a 1 is used to split the back checkers (also known as runners). Although these splitting moves leave a blot within reach of a direct hit with 5s, your opponent is unlikely to do so for fear of being hit on re-entry and forced to restart his checker back in your home board. Splitting your back checkers makes it hard for your opponent to move his own checkers without leaving them exposed to being hit.

Runners

These are checkers played from the 24-point, your back checkers as shown in the table below.

Runners		
Roll	Move	
6–5	24/13	
6–4	24/14	a
6–3	24/15	
6–2	24/16	

a) This move can also be a 2-point maker, which for a beginner is perfectly acceptable.

Modern backgammon thinking has somewhat altered these running moves in that the 6 is played 24/18 and the remaining number is moved from the mid-point (the 13-point). 6–5 played 24/13 is an exception. Although this is correct for established players, beginners are advised to stick with the 'traditional' runners until their game has reached a stage where they are competent in their checker-play and are able to recover from their 18-point blots being hit. Experiment with the 'old' and the 'new' and see what difference, if any, each one makes to winning games.

Doubles

Although **doubles** are not technically opening rolls, they are the first roll for your opponent. These, if possible, are the standard opening moves for a beginner (note that when more than one checker is moved to a particular point the move is shown as (*n*) where *n* denotes the total number of checkers moved: 2, 3 or 4).

Doubles		
Roll	Move	
6–6	24/18(2) 13/8(2)	
5–5	13/3(2)	
4–4	13/5(2)	a
3–3	8/5(2) 6/3(2)	b
2–2	13/11(2) 6/4(2)	c
1–1	8/7(2) 6/5(2)	

a) Alternative 4–4 moves are moving the back checkers 24/20(2) to make the 'golden point', with 13/9(2) with the remaining two 4s; or 24/20(2) and 8/4(2) making the (rather deep) 2-point. Generally, if your opponent has made a home-board point on his first move then playing 24/20(2) is the better move for two of the 4s.

b) Alternative 3–3 moves are making the bar-point in either table by playing 13/7(2) or 24/18(2); or any combination moving 24/21(2) and any other legal move.

c) Sometimes 2–2 is played as a golden-point maker by playing 24/20(2). This is the case when your opponent is threatening to make (or has made) his bar-point (7-point); or could well make his 5-point on his next roll.

Exercise

6   Set up the board and practise moving all the opening moves, including doubles, until you are adept at making the standard opening moves to such an extent that you don't have to think what to do but do it instinctively. Don't rush this step; take the time to learn the moves because they can often be applied at times other than the opening move. Learn about the builders and the probability of their being hit. Many 'established' players are not familiar with the opening moves and often misplay them – don't become one of them. One very important point to remember is that you have two dice and can therefore move two checkers – all too often beginners make the mistake of adding together 5 and 2 or 4 and 3 and playing them as seven, moving 13/6. Likewise with 4 and 1 or 3 and 2 being played as a five (13/8).

04

time to play a game

In this chapter you will learn:

- how to give yourself chances to turn the game around
- about the golden point, the most important point on the board
- why making the bar-point is so important
- how to make full use of the dice roll
- about the importance of timing.

Once you have mastered the opening moves it's time to play a game! This time you are on your own. Remember, try to move safely and use (safe) builders to make points and primes as you progress towards the bear-off and the finish. Keep well away from direct shots and leave as little as possible for your opponent to hit but at the same time remain flexible in your positioning of the checkers; don't pile them all on to one point. Try to have a strategy in mind, but be prepared to abandon it when things don't go the way you anticipated; always have a back-up plan!

Using these guidelines you will soon become addicted to the exciting game of backgammon – and then you'll need to study a few books of a more advanced or specific nature to improve your game. That's when you'll need to know what to do with the doubling cube – the large 'die' with the numbers 2, 4, 8, 16, 32 and 64 on it. But, until you master the art of moving, priming and bearing off the doubling cube will have to wait. You will find a little about the doubling cube later in this book, but to fully explain all its complexities could take an entire book of its own.

To get the best out of this next section it is best to read it with reference to Chapter 6, **Essential tables for winning at backgammon**. So, it's time to set up your board and play. Here are a few snippets to help you understand what needs to be done and how to do it . . .

Anchors and holding game

An anchor is a point held by you in your opponent's outer and/or home board. They are very useful in that when in your opponent's home board they inhibit his checkers from bearing into the home board and they act as safe havens for you to re-enter off the bar. Anchors on the 21- or 20-points are referred to as advanced anchors. Advanced anchors are extremely useful and desirable. Other anchors are mid-point (13-point) and bar-point (18-point) and are often part of a **holding game** – a game in which checkers are on one or more points on your opponent's side, preventing his checkers from moving freely, and are waiting for a blot as they come towards you. An example of a holding game is shown in Figure 4.1.

White's checkers on black's bar-point (white's 18-point) are holding the last four black checkers. This is a typical holding position and one that occurs in many games. White has plenty of time to play big numbers from within his own outer board and

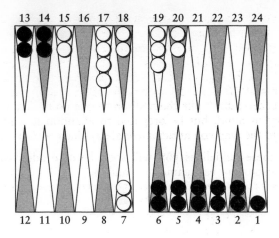

Figure 4.1

is likely to get a shot at one of the last four black checkers when black rolls sixes. Meanwhile, white is perfectly poised to form a good prime with nine decent builders, in readiness for any blot that can be knocked back on to the bar.

Backgame

When playing a **backgame,** you need to have at least two anchors in your opponent's home board, ideally on their 2- and 3-points. A backgame is one in which you have several of your checkers in your opponent's home board. This is usually a position which only experienced backgammon players will get into and should be avoided by beginners until they have gained more experience. In a backgame you have given up all hope of moving forward and want your two rear anchors to remain where they are until your opponent bears in and leaves a blot. In the holding game you are looking for the opposite – to hit a blot as soon as possible. This is a typical backgame position as shown in figure 4.2.

Very soon white will have difficulties bearing in without leaving a blot. In the meantime, black has to concentrate on forming a prime straddling his bar-point as soon as possible. Black should be aiming to make both the bar- and 4-points to enhance the possibility of keeping any white blot firmly in his home board if and when it re-enters off the bar. Already white has been denied

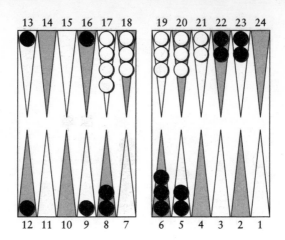

Figure 4.2

entry on to two points, his 19- and 20-points, due to the black ownership of these points; and the more points black is able to make, the harder it will be for white to re-enter.

Backgames need perfect timing and are very difficult to play and control; one big double and it could all fall apart. Backgames should be avoided if at all possible for they often result in losing a gammon (two times the stake) and, in extreme cases, backgammons (three times the stake). Many well-established backgammon players don't know how to play a successful backgame. They need a fair amount of luck to turn the game their way and a lot of knowledge to force their opponent to leave a blot at the opportune moment.

Golden point

An early anchor to aim for is the golden point (the 5-point in either table). In its purest sense the golden point refers to the 20-point, but your own 5-point (your opponent's 20-point) is of equal value; if you possess it, they can't. It was named the golden point by former world champion and author, Paul Magriel, and is recognized as the strongest point on the board. It offers great outer-board cover and ensures at least one point to re-enter off the bar. A spare checker on here is desirable so that when a blot presents itself in the outer table you are able to hit it without abandoning this valuable advanced anchor.

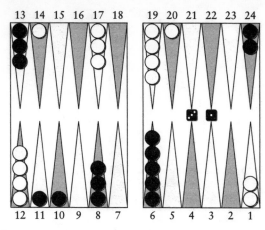

Figure 4.3

When should you make your 20-point? As soon as your opponent has opportunities to make his 5- or bar-point you should consider making the golden point. Look at the example in Figure 4.3.

Black started with 3–2 and played off his mid-point, 13/10 13/11. White responded with 2–1 and played 13/11 6/5 **slotting** the 5-point. How is black to play 3–1? There are three choices:

- make the 5-point, 8/5 6/5
- make the bar-point, 10/7 8/7
- hit on the 20-point with 24/20*. (An asterisk denotes a checker has been hit.)

Black has to hit. He has to stop white making it, even at the expense of not making his own 5-point or bar-point. Many battles are fought over the ownership of this strategic point, and in the early stages of the game being hit back isn't so harmful, so **blot-hitting contests** often erupt on both sides of the board in players' attempts to make it.

Take a look at the example in figure 4.4. This is a 'multi-roll' position, hence no dice are shown in the illustration.

Black rolls 3–1

This roll does two good things, played 10/7 8/7 it makes the valuable bar-point; or played 8/5 6/5 it makes the also valuable

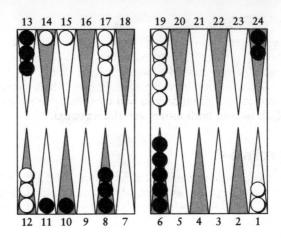

Figure 4.4

5-point. The correct play is to make the 5-point. More often than not it takes precedence over the bar-point.

Black rolls 6–1

Again, which point to make? The bar-point, 13/7 8/7; or the 5-point, 11/5 6/5? Of course, it's the 5-point. Once you've made your own 5-point it's going to remain yours until the bear-off. Although the bar-point is very important for forming a prime and stopping your opponent's runners from escaping, when given the choice of which of the two points to make the 5-point is nearly always the first one you go for.

Black rolls 4–4

There are two possible moves: make your own 5-point, 13/5(2); or your opponent's 5-point, 24/20(2) 8/4(2). This time it's the latter, your golden point. Playing off the mid-point isn't worth it because it vacates an already strong anchor and leaves a vulnerable blot. Moving off the mid-point in this position would therefore be an error. However, if one of the white runners was moved to the 20-point then 13/5*(2) is correct by a large margin (* is used in backgammon annotation to indicate when a checker is hit and placed on to the bar. In this instance, the checker on the 5-point is hit). The reason is that white now poses a threat to the 5-point and must be dealt with.

Black rolls 2–2

As a beginner, the correct play would be to make the golden point, 24/20(2). If your opponent is threatening to make his bar- or 5-point and you have the opportunity to make his 5-point, then it is generally the correct move to make. When you become more adept at backgammon you will most likely move 24/22(2) 13/11(2); however, both moves are almost equal.

Black rolls 6–3

Given the choice here (making the bar-point, 11/5 8/5 or hitting 24/14*), the correct play is to hit. Making your own bar-point is good (and an acceptable move), but stopping your opponent from making his is better.

Bar-point

Don't get the impression that the bar-point isn't important; it is. It forms the basis of a holding-prime and stops your opponent's runners from using a single die to escape. Look at this position in figure 4.5.

If black plays 13/7 9/7 he is leaving two blots (17- and 23-points) directly exposed to all but one of white's fifteen checkers, but even with the odds greatly in favour of white getting the hit,

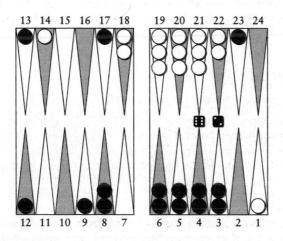

Figure 4.5

black's bar-point play is very strong. Now that white can't escape the lone runner, black won't mind being hit back on to the bar because white can't get the runner out. Eventually white may leave a blot and black could then have two white checkers back. If the 6 was played 23/17, a natural choice for a beginner, black's winning chances would be far fewer.

Building moves off the mid-point are all potential bar-point makers (and a lot of them the 5-point makers) and if at all possible the bar-point should be made as soon as a roll allows, unless it makes the 5-point first.

Primes

If, on your first few moves, you are able to make the bar- or 5-point then you will have started a prime. A prime is two or more consecutive blocks, which restrict an opponent's checkers. Primes are the key to winning at backgammon and their construction should be your main objective. If you can contain an opponent's checker(s) then you will severely restrict his ability to win the race and consequently the game.

Although the ultimate is a six-prime (six consecutive made points), over which it is impossible to escape, these are often difficult to construct and even harder to move forward. A *rolling* five-prime is more fluid and can move forward one point at a time. Also, the spare checkers in a five-prime make it very dangerous for your opponent to try and escape by slotting (moving to an open point) in front of it.

Diversification

It is impossible to make a prime without builders, so you must place your checkers in positions that enhance your chances of constructing them at every opportunity. To achieve this you must practise **diversification**. That is, you must spread your checkers out in such a manner that the majority of rolls work to your advantage. Moving off heavily stacked points (points that have more than three checkers on them) on to points with one or no checkers achieves this.

In figure 4.6 the best way to play 5–2 is from the mid-point, 13/8 and from the 6-point, 6/4. Now builders are aimed at the bar-point, the 5-point and the 2- and 1-points. Whenever possible,

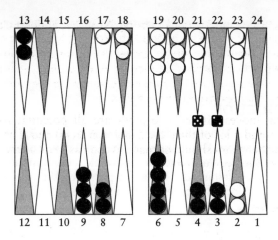

Figure 4.6

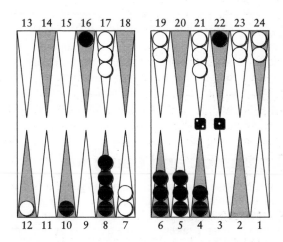

Figure 4.7

try to avoid placing checkers on points that already have any spare checkers. Keep flexible by diversifying when it is safe to do so; and always look for point-making opportunities.

What do you think is the best move here for black in the position in figure 4.7?

At the moment, black is under threat from nearly 92 per cent of white's rolls, 5s, 4s, 3s and 1s, leaving just three that miss, 6–6 and 6–2. A beginner would instinctively play 10/8 with the 2 and then either 6/5 or 5/4 with the 1. This looks good and fairly safe, but it only reduces the hits to 28, nearly 78 per cent. Black is still a big favourite to get hit.

Duplication

Sometimes you'll need to do the opposite of diversifying and do some **duplication**. Duplication is when you can leave blots that are under threat – your objective is to make your opponent's next roll work as much in your favour as possible. With this in mind, take another look at figure 4.7. Can you see a good duplication move with the 2–1?

The correct play is 22/20 16/15, duplicating 3s all round. In other words, the best roll for white is one that contains a 3 and by giving him multiple 3s you reduce your chances of being hit. Now the chances of black being hit are reduced dramatically to just 14, 39 per cent. Black has just become the favourite *not* to get hit!

Duplication is always worth seeking out, especially when the odds are stacked against you. Look at your opponent's checkers and see what threats they pose, and then look at where your checkers can move to and see if you can give your opponent fewer rolls that do you harm.

Backgammon and gammon

Not only is backgammon the name of the game it is also a score in a game or match. A **backgammon** is worth triple points and these are won when you have borne off all your checkers and your opponent hasn't taken any off and has at least one of his checkers on the bar or in your home board. A **gammon** is similar to a backgammon – you win double points if your opponent has escaped the bar or your home board but has yet to take off any checkers. If you are playing using the doubling cube then you win triple or double its current face value.

Figure 4.8 shows an example of losing a backgammon.

Black is on roll and unless he rolls 4s, 5s and 6s, or double two or double three he will be unable to escape white's home board and will lose a backgammon. He will lose the backgammon just over 72 per cent of the time.

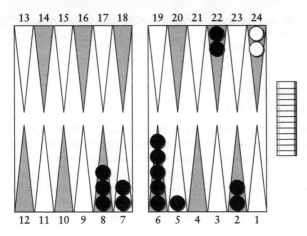

Figure 4.8

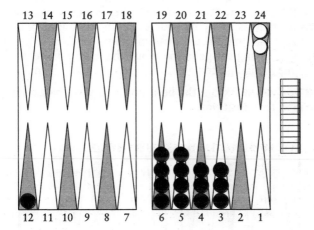

Figure 4.9

Figure 4.9 shows an example of losing a gammon.

Black is on roll and in trouble. To save the gammon and double points he needs to roll a double 3, 4, 5 or 6, or a single 6 with a 5, 4 or 3. However, if he rolls 6–2 or 6–1 he will still lose a gammon because it's not enough to have all your checkers 'home', you have to have taken at least one off to save a gammon (or backgammon) and the 2- and 1-points are empty.

More often than not, losing a backgammon is unlucky. Either you have to have a lot of checkers on the bar or roll a lot of **dancing** numbers.

Crossovers

Losing a gammon is often down to not maximizing your **crossovers**. Crossovers are when you cross over from one quadrant to another. In doing so you should waste as few **pips** as possible and aim for the nearest point in the next table. A good sound knowledge of crossovers and correct bearing-in will help reduce those gammon losses. I have often trawled the playing-rooms at tournaments and watched players failing to maximize crossovers – and then I've had to listen to them complaining about their 'bad luck' at losing a gammon!

When bearing in, aim for the top points and only fill in the lower ones if you cannot get in at least one crossover. When nearing the end of the game and you're down to your last couple of rolls, try to ensure that as many of your empty home-board points are covered as possible. In the position above (figure 4.9), black's chances of saving the gammon would have been increased if at some time he had placed a checker on the 2- or 1-points.

See if you can work out the best moves to save the gammon in these next two positions.

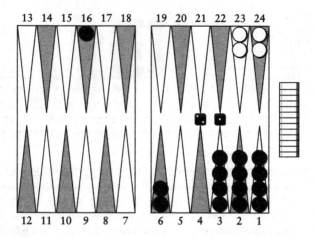

Figure 4.10

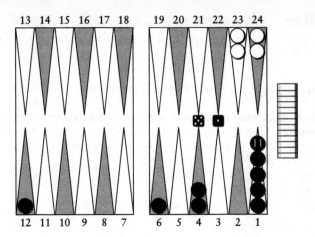

Figure 4.11

In figure 4.10, which of these two moves for black's 2–1 is the better one, and why?

- 16/15 6/4
- 16/14 6/5

In figure 4.11, which of these three moves for black's 5–1 is the better one, and why?

- 12/7 6/5
- 12/6
- 12/7 4/3

Did you spot the extra roll by playing 16/15 6/4 in figure 4.10? The extra roll is double 4. In figure 4.11 the best move giving a guaranteed gammon saver is 12/7 4/3. If you played 12/7 6/5 you'd miss out with three rolls, 3–3, 3–2; and if you'd played 12/6 then six rolls will lose you the gammon, 5–3, 5–2, 3–2.

Don't lose a gammon because you didn't see the losing rolls; keep your wits about you and look to the next roll and be certain to maximize your chances of saving gammons. Don't be the one going up to the Tournament Director and bemoaning your 'bad luck' when you fail to **save** the gammon – he won't be interested; he's heard it all before!

Blitz

Many gammons are created in the early stages of the game when a player goes for a **blitz** and hits and keeps hitting his opponent on to the bar and eventually closes him out. Blitzing isn't something I'd recommend for a beginner to have a go at but it is worth mentioning so you'll recognize one when it happens to you! However, they are fun to play and it is very satisfying when they succeed.

Often the start of a blitz follows a sequence like: white rolls 5–2 and plays 13/8 24/22. Black's reply is double 5 and he double-hits playing 8/3*(2) 5/1*(2). Typically, white dances with at least one checker and black keeps hitting them back (even leaving return direct shots off the bar). Black must commit as many checkers to the blitz as he can, which means stripping down the mid-point and bringing the checkers into play as soon as possible. Stripping down is a term used to describe moving all or nearly all the checkers off a point.

Usually, by the time you realize that the blitz is going to be successful and your opponent is going to be closed out it's too late to use the doubling cube! At this stage your opponent would be more than happy to lose a single game, so you play on for a gammon. If at a later stage it looks as if the game could turn against you, then you should be in a strong enough position to **double out** your opponent. (Doubling out is a term used to denote an opponent refusing to accept a double and conceding the game.) There are some examples of when and when not to double in Chapter 09.

Slotting

Sometimes, especially in the early stages of the game, a player will start **slotting** one of his points i.e. playing a single checker on to an empty point. More often than not this will be the 5-point or bar-point, leaving it exposed to a direct hit from the opposing runners.

Slotting is not the choice of the beginner and I recommend that you avoid slotting any points unless the odds of not being hit are well in your favour and that the odds of actually covering the slot are stacked in your favour. Many advanced players, when playing against a beginner or weaker player, will slot their 5-point with opening rolls of 4–1 (13/9 6/5) or 2–1 (13/11 6/5) or

5–1 (13/8 6/5). The 5-point blot can only be hit with a roll of 4, 41.7 per cent of the time, and the odds of covering it on the next roll are good. Generally, if your opponent slots and you roll dice that can hit it, do so!

Splitting

Too many players confuse slotting with **splitting**. Splitting is separating two checkers that are together on a point (typically the 24-point) and leaving them as blots or builders. A minor split is when you use a 1 to split the back checkers (runners); a major split is when a runner is played to a point you'd like to make – the three points that would be of use to you as advanced anchors are the golden point (20-point), or your 18-point or your 21-point. However, as a beginner you are better off staying with the minor split until you have more experience.

One checker back

A consequence of splitting is often leaving one checker back in your opponent's home board. Many beginners despair about this and try to get the lone runner to safety as soon as they can; but this isn't necessarily always the correct thing to do. Often, one lone checker is as effective as a point with two checkers on it. It can be an annoyance to your opponent and might just be your only hope of a hit and winning the game.

If you can't get the checker safe then leave it on the 24-point for as long as possible. If you move it off you'll allow your opponent to play over you and reduce your chances of sending back another of their checkers. As a beginner you would be better off keeping your two runners together, preferably on an advanced anchor, but this isn't always possible. If you do have a lone runner, make sure it's a nuisance!

Timing

One of the things you'll learn about backgammon is that if you roll big numbers you'll be around the board in no time – the problem is that often you want to go a bit slower to improve your **timing** in the race, as in this example shown in figure 4.12.

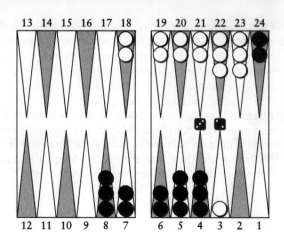

Figure 4.12

A typical beginner's play here would be to play 5/2 4/2 and make the 2-point, hoping that white doesn't roll a 6. However, this would be a very big mistake. White's timing is very poor indeed and the only way it's going to improve is if he rolls the 6 – and black must ruin white's 30 per cent chance of running with any of the 11 6s next roll.

Black's two back checkers are stuck on white's 1-point and won't escape unless white breaks his 7-point; so it's time for drastic delaying action. The correct play here (in fact it's the only realistic play) is to hit loose, moving 8/3*. Now the odds of white keeping his home-prime intact are very slim; only a roll of 6-3 will save it for him, just 5.6 per cent. White will re-enter 75 per cent of the time (27 rolls) and, unless he re-enters with 1–1, 2–2, 6-3, 3–1 or 2–1 he's going to have to break his 7-point. The chances that white will have to break up his prime is very high: nearly 78 per cent.

Too many beginners are afraid to leave blots, but often it is the correct play to make. Keep a watchful eye over the entire board and don't miss opportunities by being blinkered towards only one half of the board. Backgammon is a game of uncertainties and enigmas; often a 'rule' is turned upside down because things didn't work out the way you had planned. The best of plans can be shipwrecked on the rocks of dice and your men can be left floundering in a sea of blots and primes.

The best backgammon players are those who are quick to see a changing situation and are flexible enough and knowledgeable enough to make necessary adjustments to their game to compensate for it. The top players never complain about losing to a 'lucky' player; you make your own luck in backgammon. The big difference between good and mediocre players is that good ones play their bad rolls well; the mediocre ones play them badly and then bemoan their bad luck! Good players play against computer backgammon programs (known as 'bots'), such as Snowie™ and JellyFish™ and when they lose they learn from it – mediocre players, when they lose, denounce the bots as cheats!

05

luck in backgammon

In this chapter you will learn:

- to put the perception of luck in backgammon into perspective.

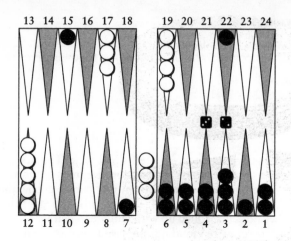

Figure 5.1

It's often said that there's a lot of luck in backgammon – and this is one reason why it's frowned upon by players whose games are based on skill; but it is this element of luck that makes backgammon so exciting and such fun to play. Games can literally change on the roll of the dice. One minute you can be cruising ahead to almost certain victory, and the next it's all gone pear-shaped and your winning position disintegrates as your opponent takes the lead.

We all have our hard-luck stories, but here's one involving my friend, Jeff Ellis, based upon a 1-point match we played at our Lincoln club.

The game got off to a bad start for me, Jeff blitzed me and I ended up with three checkers on the bar and facing a closed board except for an open 23-point. Jeff is playing as black and I am playing as white in figure 5.1 and Jeff has to play a 3–2.

As you might expect, he moved to cover the 2-point blot by playing 7/2 leaving me with three men on the bar and little chance of getting back into the game. This move gave him about 97 per cent chance of winning the game; or to put it another way, it left me with a measly 3 per cent chance of winning it!

So, there I was, three men on the bar and facing a full prime and unable to re-enter, Jeff needing to win just a single point and I said, as I put my cup and dice down to the side, 'Well, that's the end for me. No way can I win now!'

How wrong I was!

Jeff had unbelievable dice. Set up the position shown in figure 5.1 after Jeff has played 7/2 and play out the following moves:

- Black 3–3   6/3(2) 5/2(2)
- White 6–2   25/19
- Black 3–3   4/1(2)
- White 5–4   25/18 25/17
- Black 3–3   no move

I couldn't believe my luck – or Jeff's bad luck. The first 3–3 he rolled was a laugh, but not too bad for him; the second was followed by even louder laughter (from me, with a giggle about it from Jeff), amplified by my 5–4. But when he rolled a third 3–3 in a row we both just rolled up with laughter – neither of us could believe it. Tears were clouding our vision and streaming down our cheeks. There I was facing a 97 per cent chance of losing the game and it turned in my favour; I went on to win the game – against all the odds. Backgammon – what a wonderful game!

The point I am trying to make is this. This run of good/bad rolls does happen in backgammon, yet if you were black playing against a PC program or online and you got such dice you'd be convinced it was cheating! Backgammon players are always posting to newsgroups on the Internet that the dice are rigged in PC backgammon programs or on online games servers. They aren't, of course, for what would they gain by doing so? It's just that it's hard for some players to accept that bad rolls do happen. In one game I played (12 November 2005) at Live-in-London (run by the indefatigable Mike Main) I lost in the bear-off when my opponent, Michelle, rolled 6–6, 5–5, 3–3 to beat me, taking off 12 checkers in those three rolls. During the same event one player rolled seven – yes, that's not a mistake – *seven* doubles in a row to come in off the bar and to win the bear-off! Suffice it to say, no-one accused these players of cheating; but if they'd been PC programs . . .

Good backgammon players make the best moves they can and, later in this book, you'll find a match analysis that will help improve your game. Taken from the 2003 Scottish Open, it asks what play you'd make and then explains the correct play and its reasons.

06
essential tables for winning at backgammon

In this chapter you will learn:

- how to calculate the probabilities of the dice rolls and to make them favour you
- what dice rolls contain certain numbers, to enable you to make better decisions
- that two checkers are better than one when it comes to hitting an opponent or making a point
- that the key to winning backgammon is making points
- how not to lose a winning game.

Backgammon is a game of probabilities, and the more you know about them the better your game will be. A lot of players who lose at backgammon complain that the dice were against them! This isn't so; the dice are totally inanimate and have no bias towards either player – it is just the player's perception that they favour their opponent. It is essential if you want to become a good backgammon player that you study and learn (if possible) as much as you can of the following. It is this knowledge that will give you the edge over an opponent and will help you to win more games and matches. Your opponent will think you are 'lucky' and may never come to realize that your 'luck' is based upon your superior knowledge of dice probabilities.

You don't need to be a good at maths to understand the probabilities in backgammon; all you need to be able to do is add up to 36 at the most! If you can't add up to 36 then take my advice – don't take up backgammon!

Dice combinations

Detailed below are the 36 dice combinations. You don't need to remember what the rolls are, just how many there are. Remember that each roll (2–1, 5–4, 3–2, etc.) is made up of two die and either die can be the 2 or the 1. This way we get

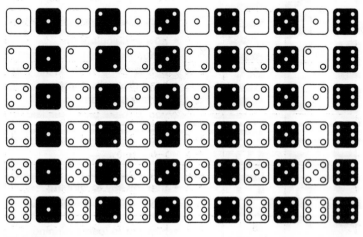

Figure 6.1

30 opening rolls, plus six doubles. Figure 6.1 illustrates the combinations.

Rolls that contain a . . .

The table below shows all the dice rolls and what numbers they contain. This is a very useful chart, and understanding the chances of certain numbers being rolled can put the dice in your favour. It's very important that you understand just how many dice rolls will contain a certain number. For example, do you know how many dice rolls contain a 1? You could look at the dice in the chart above and count them, but here's a shortcut; it's 11. Eleven is a base number for all rolls. For rolls that contain a 2, we start with 11 and add to it all dice rolls that add up to 2 but don't contain a 2, in this case, 1–1 (double one); so there are 12 rolls that contain a 2. For dice rolls that contain a 4 we start with 11 and add 2–2, 1–1, 3–1 and 1–3 to give us 15.

Rolls that contain a . . .	Total rolls	The dice combinations					
1	11	1–1	1–2	2–1	1–3	3–1	1–4
		4–1	1–5	5–1	1–6	6–1	
2	12	2–2	1–1	2–1	1–2	2–3	3–2
		2–4	4–2	2–5	5–2	2–6	6–2
3	14	3–3	1–1	2–1	1–2	3–1	1–3
		3–2	2–3	3–4	4–3	3–5	5–3
		3–6	6–3				
4	15	4–4	2–2	1–1	3–1	1–3	4–1
		1–4	4–2	2–4	4–3	3–4	4–5
		5–4	4–6	6–4			
5	15	5–5	4–1	1–4	3–2	2–3	5–1
		1–5	5–2	2–5	5–3	3–5	5–4
		4–5	5–6	6–5			
6	17	6–6	3–3	2–2	5–1	1–5	4–2
		2–4	6–1	1–6	6–2	2–6	6–3
		3–6	6–4	4–6	6–5	5–6	
7	6	6–1	1–6	5–2	2–5	4–3	3–4

Rolls that contain a . . .	Total rolls	The dice combinations
8	6	4–4 2–2 6–2 2–6 5–3 3–5
9	5	3–3 6–3 3–6 5–4 4–5
10	3	5–5 6–4 4–6
11	1	6–5 5–6
12	3	6–6 4–4 3–3
15	1	5–5
16	1	4–4
18	1	6–6
20	1	5–5
24	1	6–6

Clearly, direct rolls (rolls that are within the range of one die: 1 to 6) are the easiest to roll, with 6 being the most likely one and 1 being the least likely. So, when moving your checkers around the board, take care to minimize your chances of being hit by remembering this chart; or maximize your chances of rolling a certain number. It is very to handy to know that when your opponent leaves a blot n points away there are x number of rolls that can hit them. Again, he'll think you were lucky when in actual fact the odds were probably in your favour. The table below shows the same information but as a percentage.

% chance of rolling a specific number		
1 = 30.55%	7 = 19.44%	15 = 2.77%
2 = 33.33%	8 = 16.66%	16 = 2.77%
3 = 38.88%	9 = 13.88%	18 = 2.77%
4 = 41.66%	10 = 8.33%	20 = 2.77%
5 = 41.66%	11 = 5.55%	24 = 2.77%
6 = 47.22%	12 = 8.33%	

Rolls that hit a double shot

The next table shows how dangerous it is to expose a checker or checkers to a double hit, i.e. within the range of 1 to 6 pips away. A double shot can refer to two of your checkers that are able to hit a single opponent's checker (1 to 6 pips away) or one of your checkers able to hit two opponent's checkers (both 1 to 6 pips away). As you can see, as many as 20 (56 per cent) minimum and going up to 28 (a whacking great 78 per cent) dice rolls can hit when a checker is exposed to a double hit – something to be very wary of; and of course, the more checkers you are exposed to the greater the odds of being hit.

There are a couple of maxims often used by backgammon players; 'nearest, safest', which means that the closer a blot is to a threatening opponent the safer it is if within direct range; and 'furthest, hardest' when exposed to an indirect shot (although 12 away is worse than 11 away!).

Rolls that hit a double shot		
Numbers that hit	How many dice rolls hit and %	
6 and 1	24	66.67%
6 and 2	24	66.67%
6 and 3	28	77.78%
6 and 4	27	75.00%
6 and 5	28	77.78%
5 and 1	22	61.11%
5 and 2	23	63.89%
5 and 3	25	69.44%
5 and 4	26	72.22%
4 and 1	21	58.33%
4 and 2	23	63.89%
4 and 3	24	66.67%
3 and 1	21	58.33%
3 and 2	20	55.56%
2 and 1	20	55.56%

Being hit isn't the only use for double shots; the same odds are applied to making a point on your next roll. If you're not in too much danger of being hit by your opponent's next roll then the more chances you have of making a point the better.

To recap: the base number for rolling a single shot is 11; the base for a double shot is 20; the base for a triple shot is 27. Just remember the bases, then you can add the 'extras' when you need them.

Re-entering off the bar with one checker

We began with bearing off, and we dealt with being hit and re-entering off the bar. Of course, if you are hit – after being exposed to a double hit as above, for instance – it's as well to know what the odds are of re-entering. The inability to enter off the bar can often lead to losing the game, so it is advisable to know what rolls will enter and what won't. The next table shows the odds of re-entering with one checker against n points closed.

Re-entering one checker off the bar		
Closed points	Total number of entering rolls and %	
1	35	97.22%
2	32	61.11%
3	27	75.00%
4	20	55.56%
5	11	30.56%
6	0	This is called dancing!

Obviously, the more points closed the harder it is to re-enter, but not as hard as most beginners think! For example, often new players reckon that if three points are closed (50 per cent) then only 18 rolls (50 per cent) will re-enter; this is incorrect. Take a look at the table showing three closed points – a total of 27 rolls re-enter, that's 75 per cent, nowhere near the expected 50 per cent. In fact, with as many as four closed points you're still favourite to re-enter with 20 rolls (55.56 per cent). However, with two checkers on the bar these odds change dramatically as the next table shows.

Re-entering off the bar with two checkers

When re-entering one of two checkers or two at the same time off the bar there are huge differences: at the very best you have 25 re-entry rolls (69.44 per cent) for both checkers with just one point closed; expand this to two points closed and it drops dramatically to just 16 re-entry rolls, that's as little as 44.44 per cent. If you are facing a home board with just a measly three points closed with two on the bar, then all you have to re-enter both checkers with is nine rolls (25 per cent), which, if you reverse the maths means you don't enter 75 per cent of the time! It is important to realize that with two checkers on the bar, even re-entering one of them is far more difficult than one on its own. A single checker will re-enter against three closed points with 27 rolls, 75 per cent of the time; but, when it is joined by a second checker it drops dramatically to just 18 rolls, 50 per cent of the time.

Don't forget, while you are on the bar none of your other checkers can be moved – and that means your opponent is able to move freely without fear of you doing much to stop him. So, remember this table because it is well worth knowing just how bad/good it is to have two checkers on the bar with just a couple of points made, let alone four of five.

Entering two checkers off the bar						
Closed points	Both checkers, rolls and %		One checker, rolls and %		Neither checker, roll and %	
1	25	69.44%	10	27.78%	1	2.78%
2	16	44.44%	16	44.44%	4	11.11%
3	9	25.00%	18	50.00%	9	25.00%
4	4	11.11%	16	44.44%	16	44.44%
5	1	2.78%	10	27.78%	25	69.44%

A number of ways of making points

Earlier you learnt about builders and how important they are to forming primes and safe havens for your own checkers, so now we'll look at ways to make a point with *n* builders and, who knows, perhaps in doing so you'll put your opponent on the bar! It goes without saying that the more builders you have, the more rolls that will make points.

Number of ways to make a point				
Building points	With doubles		Without doubles	
1	1	2.78%	0	0.00%
2	4	11.11%	2	5.56%
3	9	25.00%	6	16.67%
4	16	44.44%	12	33.33%
5	25	69.44%	20	55.56%
6	36	100.00%	30	83.33%

So, don't forget the importance of builders; too few players realize their full potential and tend to stack already laden points and then find it restricts their ability to make more points. You don't need to commit this table to memory; all you need to do is square the number of building points (builders) you have available to make a point, e.g. four builders = 4×4 = 16, deduct any doubles you can't use (if any) and that's the answer. Easy, isn't it?

Now, we began this book at the end, with bearing off. So, our final table is all about the odds of getting your last two checkers off in one roll. This is a skill that too few players ever bother to attain; but one which can mean the difference between winning or losing.

Bearing off your last two checkers

Too many backgammon players don't know on what points to leave their last two checkers to have the best chance of bearing them off with one dice roll. Obviously, the lower you leave them the more rolls will do the job. Without referring to the table below, which of these two points do you think would be the better, 3 and 4, or 2 and 5?

Almost every beginner (and a lot of regular players) will go for 3 and 4, and they'd be wrong! The better one is 2 and 5 (19 rolls vs. 17 rolls), and in a game where even the slightest advantage can mean winning rather than losing, those two extra rolls are vital. Always try to end up with at least one checker on a 1 or 2 and the second as close to it as possible. Apart from 2 and 6 this is very good advice.

Bearing off your last two checkers		
Checkers on points . . .	Off in *n* rolls and %	
1 and 3	34	94.44%
1 and 4	28	77.78%
1 and 5	23	63.89%
1 and 6	15	41.47%
2 and 2	26	72.22%
2 and 3	25	69.44%
2 and 4	23	63.89%
2 and 5	19	57.78%
2 and 6	13	36.11%
3 and 3	17	47.22%
3 and 4	17	47.22%
3 and 5	14	38.89%
3 and 6	10	27.78%
4 and 4	11	30.56%
4 and 5	10	27.78%
4 and 6	8	22.22%
5 and 5	6	16.67%
5 and 6	6	16.67%
6 and 6	4	11.11%

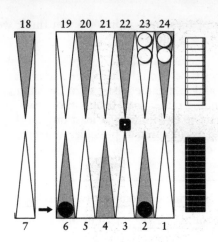

Figure 6.2

I don't suggest you commit these entire tables to memory, but if you can just remember half of them your game will improve. This is basic information that is essential to understanding the probabilities of dice rolls and their repercussions. Armed with the knowledge gleaned from this chapter you will have a tremendous advantage over an opponent who hasn't bothered to learn them. When you start making more points or hitting more blots than they do they'll think you're just lucky – let them believe that; while they attribute your skill to luck you'll always have that winning edge over them.

During the Mary Rose Trophy in February, 1996, Paul Money and Simon K. Jones were battling it out for the trophy in an exciting final. At **double match point (DMP)** Simon was on roll and he had to bear off his last two remaining checkers on his next roll to win if Paul failed to roll double 2 or better on his. If he failed to take them both off, Paul would be the winner. Simon had already played half his roll and he had a 1 left to play, as in Figure 6.2.

Simon thought about it for a while, weighing up the chances of getting both checkers off next roll, and eventually played 6/5 giving him 19 winning rolls with his checkers on his 5- and 2-points. He rolled 6/1 and lost! If he'd played 2/1 and given himself four rolls fewer he'd have won the title. You might think that sometimes it pays to be ignorant of the probabilities, but in the long term the correct play here would win more games.

07

pip-counting

In this chapter you will learn:

- that backgammon is a race and unless you know your position in that race you cannot make decisive moving decisions
- various ways of counting that tell you where you are in the race.

This is the part where you have to start counting. In fun games or those against family members, counting the pips (see below) isn't that important. However, if you want to take your game to a more serious level, then basic pip-counting techniques will pay dividends.

During many games of backgammon, knowing the pip-count can be a great advantage because many decisions throughout the game are based upon knowing it. If you don't know the pip-count when needed you're going to be at a disadvantage – you might well lose the game or match through your ignorance; it's that important!

The **pip-count** is the number of pips or spots on the dice needed to bring all checkers into the home board and to bear them off. A dice roll of 3–2 is five pips, whereas a dice roll of 6–6 is 24 pips. The average pip-count per roll is approximately eight pips. To count the pips needed you have to calculate how many pips each checker needs to move from its current point to off the board.

Just to get you in the mood, here are four pip-counting problems for you. Before going any further, cover up the text below the boards and see how long it takes you to write down the four pip-counts.

If you take more than a few seconds working out figures 7.1 and 7.2 then you really need to read this chapter; and if you take more than ten seconds each for figures 7.3 and 7.4 then keep reading.

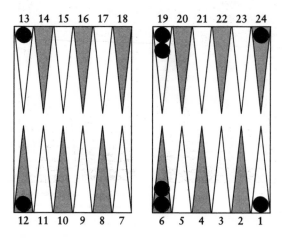

Figure 7.1

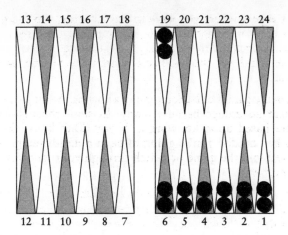

Figure 7.2

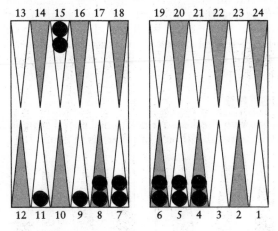

Figure 7.3

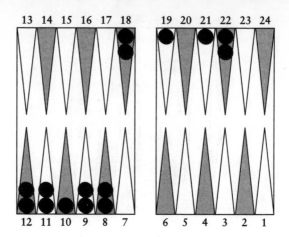

Figure 7.4

The answers are:

- Figure 7.1: 100
- Figure 7.2: 80
- Figure 7.3: 110
- Figure 7.4: 210

Did you spend all your time counting every checker on every point and adding them all together? This is called the 'direct method' and is very tedious. Well, you didn't have to do it that way; there are several short-cuts to assist you in this important task. One of the easiest counting short-cuts is opposites.

Opposites

This is when two checkers are positioned exactly opposite each other in the same table (home or outer) as in figure 7.5.

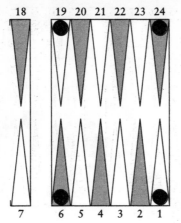

Figure 7.5

Wherever two checkers are lined up as above they will always have a pip-count of 25 (19 + 6, 24 + 1); it doesn't matter what points they occupy, it will always be 25 pips. If there is more than one checker on each point then each opposing pair counts as 25. Now, look back at Figure 7.1 and you'll see that the quickest way to count is that we have three blocks of opposites, two of which total 50 (1 + 24 and 13 + 12) and one block that totals 50 (19 + 6 × 2); therefore, quick as a flash we see that the pip-count is 100. In fact, when you've finished this chapter and come to understand pip-counting short-cuts you'll have worked it out as 4 × 25 = 100 in about three seconds at the most. This is much faster than 24 + 19 + 19 + 13 + 12 + 6 + 6 + 1 = 100.

Another short-cut method for quick counting is blocks.

Blocks

This is when an even block of checkers are used to determine a base number and then adjustments made to compensate for gaps or vacant points. 'Even' in this instance refers to the number of checkers on each point and not to the number of points in the block. Look at figures 7.6, 7.7 and 7.8.

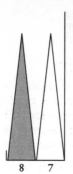
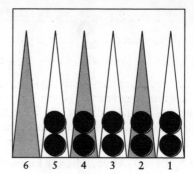

Figure 7.6

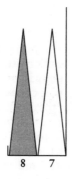
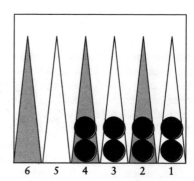

Figure 7.7

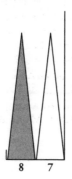
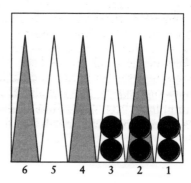

Figure 7.8

A block of ten checkers will always total 30 pips.

A block of eight checkers will always total 20 pips.

A block of six checkers will always total 12 pips.

As can be seen from the point numbers, these totals only work for checker blocks connected to the 1-point. When the blocks are higher up the board, adjustments have to be made. Whenever there is a vacant point below the block, the pip-count is increased by as many checkers in the block as there are vacant points.

Look at figure 7.9. As you already know, a block of ten checkers equals a pip-count of 30 pips.

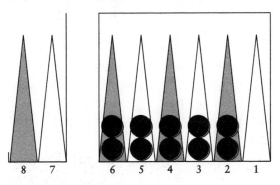

Figure 7.9

With just the 1-point vacant, the pip-count of 30 is increased by 1 × 10 (vacant point(s) × checkers in block) = 10 + 30 = 40. So, very quickly you can count any block anywhere. If the block had been eight and there were two vacant points then the count would have been 2 × 8 (vacant points × checkers in block) = 16 + 20 = 36 pips. So, for each vacant point add the number of checkers in the block to the base number. This is true of blocks straddling the bar or the outer tables – anywhere you can find a block of checkers. Did you also spot that in figure 7.9 the block could have been counted more quickly by piling all the checkers on to the centre point, the 4-point? More on this method later.

Take another look at figure 7.2. You should now see this as two separate blocks. One of opposites (19 + 6) and one of a block of ten (5- to 1-point). The opposites total 50 (2 × 25) and the block totals 30; therefore we can calculate very quickly 80 pips.

Now look again at figure 7.3. Quite clearly we have a block of ten that will have a base of 30, plus three vacant points with 10 pips = 60 total for the block; but how do we calculate the remaining four checkers? To make things a little clearer, let's have a look at a section of figure 7.3 on its own.

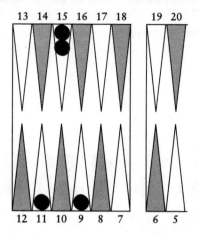

Figure 7.10

In figure 7.10 we can now see an offset opposite. The single checkers on the 11- and 9-points form a triangle with the two checkers on the 15-point; this is akin to moving the two single checkers on to the 10-point and adding up the opposites to a total of 50 pips, making a grand pip-count of: 60 (block) + 50 (opposites) = 110 pips.

When doing a pip-count, look for blocks and opposites as these are the easiest of checkers to count. Offset opposites are sometimes a little 'out of sync' inasmuch as you might need to make a mental adjustment now and again to contrive one, but generally this isn't too hard after a little practice.

Look once again at figure 7.4 and see if you can work out the pip-count using blocks and opposites. Did it take a long time? Couldn't do it? It is a little cumbersome using blocks; but there is a much simpler way to count them that I touched on above.

Centre-point block-counting method

As the name implies, blocks are counted using the central point of the block (odd blocks are easiest, but even ones can be calculated with a little effort). Look at figure 7.9 again.

First we need to identify the central point; in this easy example it is quite obviously the 4-point. Now, imagine levelling off all the checkers on to the one central point. Anyone can multiply ten by four, can't they? So, just by identifying the central point and using your brain a little you can count blocks in the twinkling of the eye.

As I said, this method works easily for odd blocks, but even ones require a little more brain power – but don't panic; it's not that hard! Look at figure 7.11 to see how to count an even centre-point block.

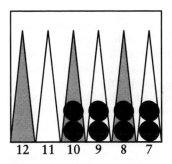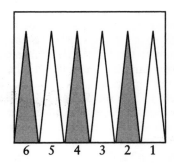

Figure 7.11

The central point for this block is 8.5; so just multiply the checkers (8) by 8.5 to get 68, Simple, isn't it? Mind you, this example is as quick using the block method (20 + 48 = 68), but I'm sure you get the idea. With a little practice and lateral thinking odd blocks, even blocks and blocks with gaps can all be counted quickly using the central-point method.

The running total difference

Finally, figure 7.12 shows one method that seems very simple until you're hit and placed on the bar. Look at the starting position.

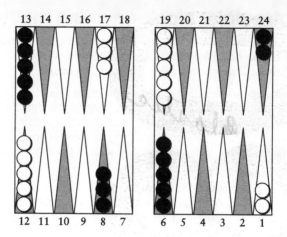

Figure 7.12

Don't bother doing a pip-count; trust me, the pip-count for each player is 167 pips. All you have to do in this method is keep a running total of the difference between you and your opponent. For example, you roll 3–1, therefore you are four pips ahead; your opponent rolls 6–5 and you drop down to seven pips behind; you roll 5–5 and go into the lead with 13 pips; and so on and so on. Now, you might just think that this is by far the best method you've come across; it's so easy, all you need to do is add and subtract, and the biggest number you'll have to deal with is 24. Don't fall for it! It is nigh impossible to keep up to date; being hit back on to the bar or dancing with half a roll will both complicate matters – but if you don't believe me, have a go.

In conclusion, there are other short-cuts to pip-counting, but for the moment there should be enough here for you to develop a system that suits you. No system is better than the others; the best system is perhaps a hybrid of one or more methods – find the one that suits you the best and then practise, practise, practise. It might seem like a tedious thing to be doing, but it isn't done constantly, only when you need to know the racing positions. Backgammon players who carry out pip-counts lose fewer games because they know exactly where they are in the race in relation to their opponent – another edge. During a game, keep an eye open for blocks, patterns and so on, and use the opportunity to do a pip-count; it will be worth it in the long run.

08

keeping count

In this chapter you will learn:

- ways to remember the pip-count without resorting to pen and paper.

So, you've mastered pip-counting, but have you worked out how to keep the score in your head while counting your opponent's pips? This is perhaps the hardest thing to do; you get your own pip-count, you get your opponent's pip-count, and then you find you've forgotten your own pip-count! Because it is illegal to write down the pip-count, devious methods have been invented by some clever people using an aid that no-one can take away from you – your hands! Here are three examples.

Palm-up and palm-down

Place your right hand face down on your leg and count 1 to 5, with 1 being your thumb; turn your hand over and count 6 to 9 starting with the little finger and ignoring your thumb. Do the same for the tens with your left hand. To record your pip-count all you need do now is identify your tens finger and your singles finger and there you are. Perfectly legal.

The curly finger

Count one side, and then store the answer on your fingers in your lap to save having to remember it while counting the other side. It's really easy to do this. Record the tens on your left hand, one finger down for 10, two for 20 etc.; one down curled up for 60, two for 70, etc. Same for the units on your right hand. Once again, to record your pip-count all you need do now is identify your tens finger and your singles finger and there you are. Another easy one.

The board and finger

This sounds like one of those trendy pubs that have mush-roomed up in the last few years, but it is a really easy method and you don't have to contort your fingers in the process. Quite simply, make use of the points on the board. Use a thumb to indi-cate tens and a finger to indicate units; so for a pip-count of 86 place your left thumb near the 8-point (80) and your right finger near the 6-point (6), and there you are, 86. When the count is greater than 129 (thumb near 12-point, finger near 9-point) then use your knuckle to indicate tens and keep the finger for the units. With this method there isn't any need to cross your hands over for awkward counts just keep fingers for units and thumbs or knuckles for tens and you can go up as high 252 (knuckle near 24-point, finger near 12-point). I am claiming to be the inventor of this method simply because I thought it up and I haven't seen it published elsewhere!

So, we are now at the end of this section on pip-counting. If you've followed and understood what I've been on about, counting over the board will become second nature to you. It really isn't difficult and is very worthwhile – especially if you know how to do it and your opponent doesn't. Before we finish, here are a few tips and extra short-cuts.

Tips

- When pip-counting, start at the high end; it's easier to do 3 × 23 and then add on 4 × 4 than do 4 × 4 and then add on 3 × 23.
- Two checkers on each home-board point total 42 pips. Or, put another way . . .
- A 6-prime block of two checkers per point in your home board is 42 pips.
- Checkers on the bar are 25 pips each.
- One checker on each of the 13- and 7-points total 20 pips.
- Your opponent's 5-point is 20 pips away.
- Your opponent's bar-point is 18 pips away.
- Keep calm when counting and don't get distracted.
- Practise, practise, practise.

09

the doubling cube

In this chapter you will learn:

- what the doubling cube is
- when to double and when not to double
- to work out the doubling strategy based on position, race and threat
- not to let your opponent roll big doubles and win the game
- about the Crawford rule.

Without doubt the little cube with the 64 on it that comes with every backgammon set is the hardest part of the game to master. Not one single backgammon player in the world can claim to know everything about when to and when not to use the doubling cube. Even so-called experts have differing opinions and backgammon software with their algorithms can't always agree. All I can do at this level is to introduce the cube to you and give you some idea of its correct use.

What is a doubling cube?

A doubling cube is used in either money games or in tournaments where players are playing matches of a set number of games and it is used to double the stake or the number of points being played for. Invented in the USA in the 1920s, it has changed the game dramatically and has been the one addition to the modern game that has had the most impact.

It starts out at the side of the board in the centre, with the 64 facing up. The 64 signifies that the stake or game being played for is currently 1. Either player can **double** his opponent, during his turn and prior to rolling the dice, and increase the stake to 2 points. This is done by picking up the cube, turning the '2' face up and passing it to your opponent by placing it on the playing surface in front of him in the table on your right-hand side, saying words to the effect, 'I double to two.' The opponent then has two choices:

- He can refuse to accept the double and lose a single point, saying words to the effect, 'I drop.'
- He can accept the increased stake by saying words to the effect, 'I take' and then placing the cube on his side of the table with the 2 face up.

Once you have passed over the doubling cube and your opponent has accepted it, you no longer have access to it; the stake has now doubled. Now the cube can only be used by its new owner. If he decides at some later stage of the game that he would like to increase the stake from 2 to 4 (re-doubling) then the whole double and take/drop process starts all over again. This time, if the double is dropped then the loss is two points and the game ends, otherwise it is taken and the new stake is 4 points. There isn't a limit to the value of the cube but realistically in matches to 11 points (for example) it is unlikely to go too high. In money games it isn't unusual to see 64 and even higher (special cubes going up to 1024 are available!).

The doubling cube is a powerful weapon and one that you should not hand lightly to your opponent. Once you relinquish it, you must always be prepared for it to be used against you. At its higher stake the cube becomes more difficult to accept, especially in a tournament, and therefore it should be used with caution. Don't offer it across too early – a mistake made by many players, and one that they often live to regret.

The 25 per cent and 10 per cent rules

It is argued that the only reason a player would double the stake is because he thinks he has a better chance of winning the game, so why would anyone want to take such a double? If it were that simple then the cube wouldn't have had the huge impact on the game that it has. If a player to whom the cube is offered calculates that he has (approximately) a 25 per cent chance of winning the game then he should take it – thus the 'Jacoby Paradox' informs us! Attributed to Oswald Jacoby, a world-renowned player and author, it has been proved that if you are the underdog but have no less than 25 per cent then you should take. Look at the simple, two-roll finish shown in figure 9.1.

Black is on roll and will fail to win if he rolls a 1, unless it is double-one. He is favourite to win this game at 72.2 per cent; therefore, white, who will be off next roll, has a 27.8 per cent chance of winning. This is greater than 25 per cent so white should take.

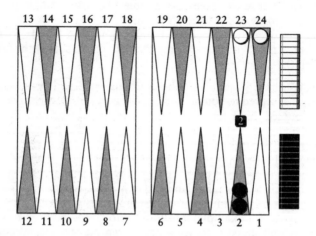

Figure 9.1

Here's how it works out over 100 games:

If white drops every cube   −100 games

If white takes:

loses 72.2 × 2-cube   −144.4
wins 27.8 × 2-cube   +55.6

Overall   −88.8

Therefore, over 100 games white's losses are reduced to a little under 89 by taking the cube as opposed to dropping it each time.

Although this is a simple example, the 25 per cent rule applies in more complex positions; however, when it comes to re-cubes then it generally drops to about 22 per cent. Also, the cube is often offered much earlier than in this position. Of course, the 25 per cent rule is a general rule and it is possible to have a double/take position with 20 per cent. Here's an example in figure 9.2.

Black offers the 2-cube to white. It is approximately 80 per cent to black and 20 per cent to white, yet white can take. This is because it is possible that black might roll one of the ten 1s that fail to get both checkers off. After black fails to take both checkers off, white then has a re-cube to four, which black should accept, the odds being 72 per cent to 28 per cent in black's favour. It is this **recube vig**, or ownership of the cube, that enables white to take and re-cube.

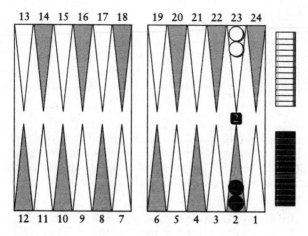

Figure 9.2

PRaT

Backgammon author and player, Robin Clay (who died in November 2000) taught me the **PRaT** method of calculating double/take positions. The acronym stands for **P**osition, **R**ace and **T**hreat. Let's look at figure 9.3, where black is on roll. Should black double? Should white take?

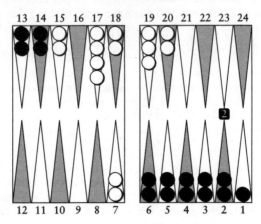

Figure 9.3

- **Position:** Black has a good home-board prime, but has four checkers in white's outer board. White has a very poor home board, but the two checkers on black's 7-point are in a strong holding position.
- **Race:** Black 95, White 130. Black leads by 35 pips and is on roll, which is worth approximately another eight pips.
- **Threat:** Black doesn't have any real threats except rolling doubles to clear his last two checkers. White is very well placed to hit any blots black might leave if he rolls a 6 and has to move one of his last four checkers.

Black is lacking in two of the three; his position might look good but the last four checkers are badly placed; nor does he pose much of a threat to white. In fact, it is white who poses the greater threat with his last two checkers bearing down from the black bar-point. Therefore, black should not double, and if he does, white should take.

Generally in PRaT positions, if you have a clear advantage in two of the three areas then it is OK to offer the cube; being at a disadvantage in all three usually signifies a drop.

For beginners, the pip-count can be used to assess doubling positions. Here the 10 per cent rule is applied. If your pip-count lead is greater than 10 per cent of your opponent's pip-count, then you should double; if it is less, do not double. For example: your pip-count = 142, your opponent's pip-count = 160, your lead is 18 pips, which equates to 12.7 per cent making it a double. When deciding to take a first double then the 10 per cent rules moves to between 12 per cent and 12.5 per cent, making this example a marginal drop when based purely upon a pip-count difference. It needs to be pointed out that these are general rules and are not hard and fast; but when combined with PRaT they are a good guide.

Too good to double

There will be times when you are **too good to double** and you'll want to play on for a gammon. One way to assess the position is to become your opponent for a while and take a look at the board from his point of view. If you then think to yourself as your opponent that you're in real danger of losing a gammon, don't offer him the easy way out and ship across the cube – keep it to yourself or leave it in the middle. Look at figure 9.4.

White has two checkers on the bar and his third blot is under threat, added to which, black has 16 rolls (44.4 per cent) that will close off the 2-point. White is in very great danger of losing a

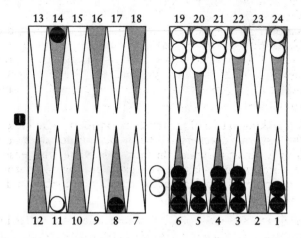

Figure 9.4

gammon and would dearly love to drop any cube and reduce his losses. Black should play on for the gammon.

Double them out

Also keep a sharp eye open for times when you want to **double out** your opponent from the game. These are occasions, more often than not in no-contact positions, where you have a good racing lead (perhaps for which you'll need a pip-count to establish by how much) and your opponent will require doubles to catch you up in the race. Failing to double in these positions will allow your opponent to have chances to roll the doubles required and perhaps lose you the game. For example, in figure 9.5 black, on roll, should double his opponent out.

The only way white is going to win now is if he rolls big doubles. Almost 17 per cent of all rolls are doubles, half of them double-four or greater. White has nothing to lose by hoping to roll one or more – therefore black should double white out before he has any chances to roll them. Many beginners fail to see the logic of doubling out when in a straight race winning position – and subsequently they end up losing games they could have won (and then bemoan their 'bad luck' to the Tournament Director).

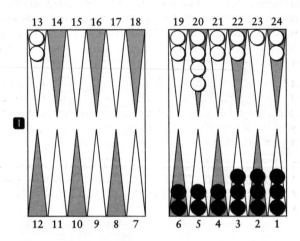

Figure 9.5 .

The Crawford rule

An American, John Crawford, invented this rule for the doubling cube. It is used in match play and the rule is that when a player reaches match point (within one point of winning the match), the cube cannot be used by either player for that one game and should be removed from the board and placed at the side. The leading player now has one game in which to win the match without either player using the cube before it is brought back into play the very next game if he fails. In any subsequent games, the cube should be replaced on the board and can be used by the trailer prior to any legal throw except the opening roll. Many beginners who are behind in the match forget that after the Crawford rule has passed they *should double immediately* before their first roll (unless it is the first of the game). The reason for this is that the leader needs only one point to win the match, and the trailer needs to maximize his wins. It doesn't matter if the trailer loses one point or two, the game is lost if their opponent wins any more games.

The Jacoby rule

This rule relates to money play and it states that gammons or backgammons only count as one point unless the cube has been taken during the game. The idea behind it is to cut down on longer games where one player plays on for a gammon or backgammon; to do so when the **Jacoby rule** is in force is unnecessary. As you might have guessed, this rule is named after its 'inventor', Oswald Jacoby.

For most beginners, the doubling cube is a complex instrument and one to be avoided if at all possible – but to avoid it is to turn your back on the modern game. There are many books available nowadays that deal with the doubling cube in depth, and any serious player has at least one in their collection.

One final thought: don't miss out on a doubling opportunity. Before every roll, your own and your opponent's, think, 'Can I cube?' or, 'Can I take a cube?' If you miss an opportunity it could prove costly in the long run.

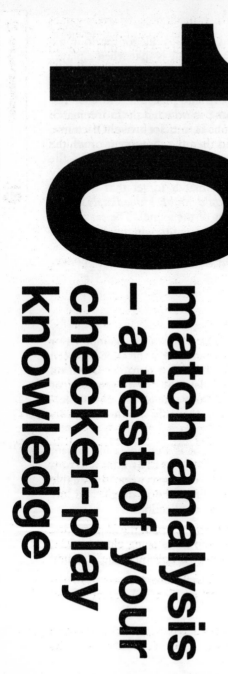

10

match analysis – a test of your checker-play knowledge

In this chapter you will learn:

- that one of the best ways to improve your game is to study games that have been recorded and analysed by a computer program

One of the best ways to improve your game is to study games recorded and analysed by the computer program, Snowie™. This chapter uses a match from the finals of the 2003 Scottish Open. Before we begin the analysis it is important that you fully understand the notation used in describing moves and actions around the board.

Each board is shown from black's position and the movement of the black checkers in all positions is anticlockwise. Of course, when white's moves are featured then the movement of white's checkers is clockwise.

Terminology

Dice rolls: Shown as 6–4 or 4–2 or 1–1. Always in pairs. Some publications show them as 64, 42.

Movement: A roll of 6–4 for black is shown as 6–4: 24/18 13/9. One checker is moved from the 24-point to the 18-point, and the other checker moved from the 13- to the 9-point, in an anticlockwise direction. If the move were for white then it would be exactly the same but the white 24-point is the black 1-point and the white 13-point is the black 12-point and the checkers would move clockwise. This reversal of point numbers for your opponent's moves can at first seem very difficult to understand, but with practice and familiarity it will become second nature. Once you understand the moves and the point from which the move is made and to what point it is moved you'll find the annotation quite easy to cope with. When doubles are moved (*n*) is used to show how many checkers were moved, e.g. 2–2: 13/11(2), 6/4(2).

If, when making a move, an opponent's blot is hit then the move is shown thus: 6–4: 8/2* 6/2 where * denotes a hit on the 2-point and the second move 6/2 makes the point. After being hit the blot is placed on the bar (the 25-point).

The bar: The bar (central divider) is referred to as the 25-point and checkers re-entering the game are shown as being played 25/21, where the checker is re-entered in this example on to the 21-point.

Bearing off: Checkers are borne-off to 0 (zero) and are shown as 5/0 2/0 where checkers are taken off the 5- and 2-points following a roll of 5–2.

Doubling cube: Some of the positions will feature the doubling cube, the large die with numbers 2, 4, 8, 16, 32 and 64 on its faces. This tutorial does not deal with the complexities of the doubling cube. Some of the complexities of the cube are dealt with in Chapter 9 and you are recommended to seek dedicated books on the cube.

The match

The Scottish Open 2003 final saw two outsiders playing for this major title. Peter Chan (white) and Rosey Bensley (black) had both beaten all before them and had rightly earned their places at the final table. Without taking anything from either player, at the start of the competition you could have got some very good odds on this pair being finalists. Certainly on paper and according to the ranking scores there were far 'better' players in the field. In fact, Rosey beat one of the favourites, John Slattery (a former European Champion), in her first round!

Snowie™ (see Glossary) rated them both overall as beginners in a match that had 80 errors, 32 of which were blunders. I have taken a look at those blunders using Snowie™ Pro4 and I've attempted to direct the two finalists towards the correct play, at the same time pointing out (in my opinion) why their plays were incorrect.

In this tutorial I have taken the positions only and not shown the entire match. At the top of each position I have shown the player and his or her colour along with his or her match score. The actual move played is shown beneath the dice roll followed by its Snowie™ position. Finally, the 'advice' is shown in *italics*. Cover up the text after each position and decide upon your own move before revealing the analysis.

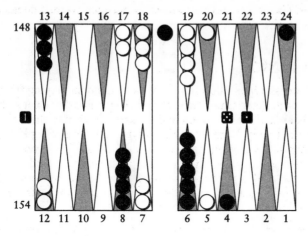

Figure 10.1

Black to play 5–1

51: 25/20* 4/3 (Snowie's position 3)

The actual play here of 25/20* 4/3 is too passive. It is far better to go for the double hit by playing 25/20* 6/5* – it will stop white making the black 5-point, and at the same time increase black's chances of making white's 5-point. Although it leaves two blots, white's home board is very easy to come in on.

Placing two checkers on the bar, frequently referred to as 'two in the air', is often the correct play. It is always possible that one or both checkers may not re-enter and this will give you time to carry out your moves around the board in the knowledge that few, if any, rolls from your opponent will harm you.

Chan (w) : 0 Bensley (b) : 0

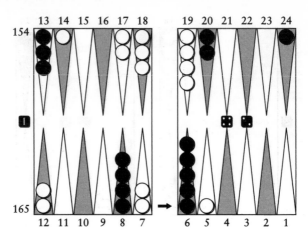

Figure 10.2

Black to play 4–2

42: 20/14* (Snowie's position 3)

Hitting from the 20-point is very wrong here. It vacates the most valuable anchor on the board and gives white a good few chances to make a similar anchor – something that black does *not* want to happen. Black needs to make another point here, and therefore making an important home-board point by playing 8/4 6/4 is best. At the moment, hitting without any more home-board points is a waste of a good roll.

Rarely hit from the 20-point unless you have a spare checker to do so. It is too valuable to vacate lightly. After rolling the dice ask yourself two things: Can I make a point? Can I hit a blot? If you can do both then look at the consequences of each action and assess the better of the two. Home-board points are nearly always good points to have – without them you'll find it very difficult to keep an opponent on the bar.

Chan (w) : 0 Bensley (b) : 0

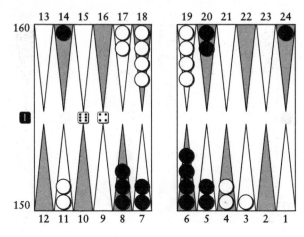

Figure 10.3

White to play 6–4

64: 21/11* (Snowie's position 3)

Note that this is the first position to show one of white's moves. Remember that his 24-point is black's 1-point; therefore he is playing off black's 4-point, his own 21-point and hitting on black's 14-point, his own 11-point.

Black's last four checkers will have to start moving around soon, so hitting one back 21/11* will only delay her and at the same time vacate the only anchor in her home board. The better play by a long chalk is to keep all the occupied points intact and play the spare checker off the 22-point, 22/12. Getting hit back isn't that big a deal at the moment; white occupies a very good advanced anchor and therefore shouldn't have too much difficulty getting in off the bar.

Don't break off good anchors for a useless hit. At the moment, white's home board has just one point (and that was one he started with!) and therefore hitting the blot on his 11-point won't do much harm to black.

Chan (w) : 0 Bensley (b) : 0

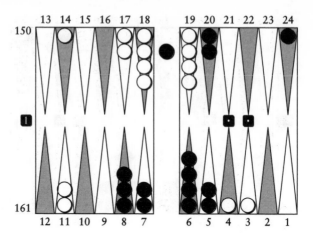

Figure 10.4

Black to play 1–1

11: 25/23 5/4*(2) (Snowie's position 5)
Well, it's happened. Re-entry and hits. But, the passive play of
25/23 5/4*(2) doesn't really harm white. It would have been far
better to go for the double hit, 25/24 6/4* 4/3*. White has left
three blots on and black should be looking to scoop them all up.
If you can, always try to put two in the air.

*Two in the air (remember figure 10.1?) and aim to make another
home-board point. Playing 5/4*(2) also vacates the valuable 5-
point and places a gap in a 4-prime. Black needs to make some
home-board points and should take this opportunity to start
making one of them.*

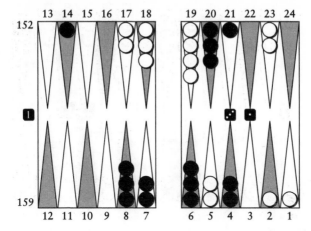

Figure 10.5

Black to play 3–1

31: 6/2* (Snowie's position 6)

Playing 6/2* only gives white more chances of getting another checker on the 20-point anchor, without which it becomes stripped if a blot presents itself. Black should play the safe 8/4 and threaten the two blots on her 2- and 1-points, at the same time leaving the blot on her 14-point vulnerable to only 5–4 and 6–3 – this would leave white with a 'free' six off the bar to hit back with. The black blot on white's 4-point isn't in too much danger – at the very best white might point on it but that'll still leave 27 re-entry rolls

Try to keep out of reach of an opponent's rolls. If you can't do that, at least see if you can get a reasonable return hit off the bar.

Chan (w) : 0 Bensley (b) : 0

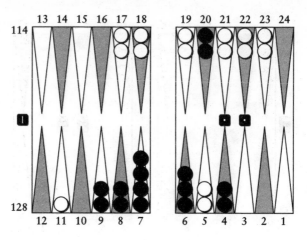

Figure 10.6

Black to play 1–1

11: 9/8(2) 4/3(2) (Snowie's position 11)
White is running out of time here. He needs to roll 5s or 6s to
escape the back checkers or else his prime will most likely **crunch**
up. With this in mind, black should keep holding the prime intact
and simply shift points from her 4-point to her 2-point. Instead,
she moves off the 9-point with two checkers and shifts to the 3-
point. This play greatly increases white's escaping chances –
something that white wants desperately and is very happy to see.

*Don't break a holding-prime if you can move behind instead. It
might look as if playing to the 2-point is a bit too deep, but the
alternative of moving off the 9-point is far worse. Once white
escapes his last two runners he'll be well poised to knock back the
last remaining black checkers should the opportunity present itself.*

Chan (w) : 2 Bensley (b) : 0

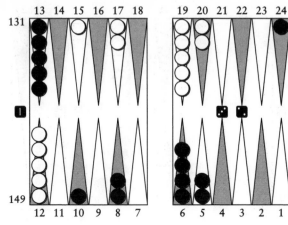

Figure 10.7

Black to play 3–2

32: 8/5 24/22 (Snowie's position 16)

The black back checker looks like a liability, but it isn't. It is an asset, being her only chance of hitting a blot. Therefore, it is of more use on the 24-point than anywhere else for the moment. Black played 8/5 24/22, which allowed white to play 4s and 5s over the blot to the 22-point, at the same time breaking off a point for no gain whatsoever. The correct play here is to move 13/10 to make a building point and slot the 4-point. If the back checker does hit a blot later, home-board points will be vital in keeping it on the bar; at the moment neither player has made much of an attempt at making a decent home board.

Try to make as many home-board points as you can when you have lost your opponent's runners; you'll need to keep them on the bar or in your home board should you get the hit later. For this reason black's runner on white's 1-point is her only hope of getting a hit; white will be trying to avoid leaving a blot. Black could do with another checker back and try to make an anchor, but the likelihood of this happening with the checkers in the position above is very slim.

Also, do not waste a move by piling checkers on to an already established point, as with black's move of 8/5; slotting the 4-point and playing 13/10 would have greatly increased the chances of making the 4-point.

Chan (w) : 3 Bensley (b) : 1

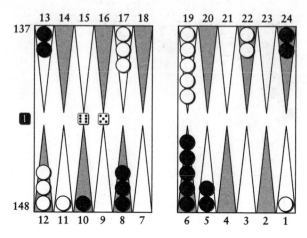

Figure 10.8

White to play 6–5

65: 14/8 13/8 (Snowie's position 3)
White decides to load his 8-point by playing 14/8 13/8 (remember, black's 11- and 12-points), which is very cumbersome and unnecessary. If the 14-point blot must be moved then it should be moved to the 9-point. The correct move is a simple runner 24/13 to the mid-point. This only leaves black 11 shots to hit the blot (2s), which, if it's missed, will put white in a good position.

If it is possible to leave indirect builders then do so in preference to stacking an existing point. It's a good idea to have a spare checker on a point as a builder, but in this instance white is adding another two. Almost anything else is better than stacking – certainly when the home board is so poor. In most cases, the only time you should stack is when it's unavoidable and no better move presents itself.

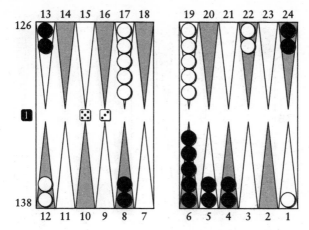

Figure 10.9

White to play 5–3

53: 13/8 13/10 (Snowie's position 2)
White decides to completely abandon his lone runner and move
13/8 13/10. Now the poor back checker has to run 14 pips to
safety – a tall order. It might look ugly, but the only alternative
is to play two checkers to the 3-point, 8/3 5/3. The mid-
point anchor is too valuable to give up and these two points are
already loaded.

*Never leave a checker behind to fend for itself, always try to have
at least one point on which it can land safely. Keep in communication – and keep as near as possible. As I said above, stack only
when it is unavoidable. Technically, stacking here is unavoidable
inasmuch as the alternative, abandoning the runner, isn't acceptable.*

Chan (w) : 3 Bensley (b) : 1

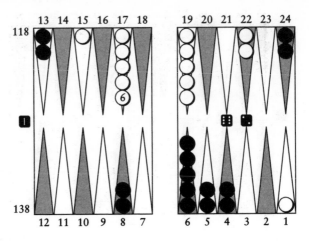

Figure 10.10

Black to play 6–2

62: 13/5 (Snowie's position 4)
Black has two objectives here:

- to escape the runners
- to stop the white back checker from escaping.

Playing 13/5 will not achieve either. Sixes will be rolled to escape the lone white checker – and two of them will hit. At the moment, white has a two-point board with gaps and therefore now is the time to poke your head out and run, 24/18 18/16. If you get hit back by one of the 11 rolls that contain a 1, it could well turn out to be in your favour with the establishment of an advanced anchor.

Try not to play checkers past a point you want to make. Keep them active for as long as you can. Playing 13/5 might be a good builder for the 3-point, but the priority here should be trying to make the bar-point.

Chan (w) : 3 Bensley (b) : 3

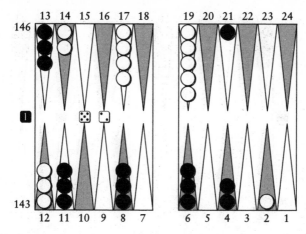

Figure 10.11

White to play 5–2

52: 13/6 (Snowie's position 5)
The last thing the 6-point needs here is another checker. Five is
too many, six is far too many–but white doesn't think so! Instead,
moving 8/3 helps lessen the load on the 8-point and aids the
making of the 3-point; moving 13/11 gives a spare checker in the
outer board for hitting/pointing if needed.

*When you can't find a point-making or blot-hitting move, try to
shift a few checkers off the stacked points and look for point-
making opportunities. The play of 13/11 will give black a chance
to hit with any 6, but many of the 6s will also make a good point
elsewhere: 6–1, bar-point or 5-point; 6–4, bar-point or hit on the
2-point; 6–3, 5-point; 6–6, bar-point and 5-point.*

Chan (w) : 4 Bensley (b) : 3

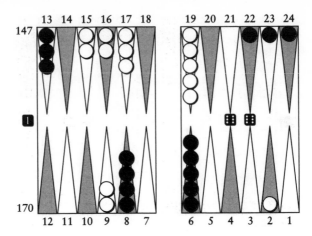

Figure 10.12

Black to play 6–6

66: 13/7(2) 8/2*(2) (Snowie's position 3)
Hitting on the 2-point is clearly correct, but taking two off the mid-point to cover the bar-point only gives up the valuable blocking mid-point for a small gain. It is far better to keep the mid-point and bring another builder around from the 24-point, 24/12. White might hit the 12-point blot but, with a one-point board, this isn't a problem for black.

Don't give up blocking points to make others unless the point you're making is worth having and risk free. So far in this game black has achieved little and now has a chance to improve her position. If white were to hit off the bar with a 3 (any except 6–3) it could well work in black's favour. She could end up with an advanced anchor or she could send another white checker back on to the bar with a 1 or a 3 of her own.

Chan (w) : 4 Bensley (b) : 3

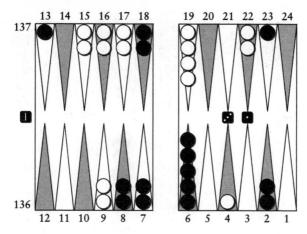

Figure 10.13

Black to play 3–1

31: 23/20 13/12 (Snowie's position 8)
White is going to find it difficult to make another point or play into his home board because of the black blot on his 2-point. This annoying blot is black's best hope of a hit. If it's moved up to the 20-point it'll allow white to play over it and safely home without risk. Therefore, black's play of 23/20 13/12 is wrong. At the moment, neither side has an home board worth a jot, and therefore hits to the bar aren't so painful. Now is the time for black to make the important 5-point, playing 8/5 6/5. It looks dangerous, but with an almost even race it isn't.

The 5-point is a point for life! And don't allow your opponent to make safe plays over your head . . . unless you want them to! Did you spot the added 'benefit' of making the 5-point? Although black has left two blots on they are each four pips away – duplication! Even the blot in white's home board is four pips away from white's spare checkers on his 6-point. If you did spot this duplication then you are well on your way to becoming a good backgammon player; if you didn't, don't despair, you haven't read the whole book yet!

Chan (w) : 4   Bensley (b) : 3

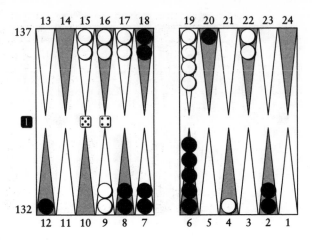

Figure 10.14

White to play 5–4

54: 21/16 6/2 (Snowie's position 2)

Black's home board is too poor not to take advantage of. Pointing 10/5* 9/5 is far superior to the safe-played move of 21/16 6/2. The safe play doesn't achieve much, whereas the attacking play makes a great point and it is possible that black could dance, further enhancing the play.

Take advantage of a poor home board to make points and/or hit. White will have three decent points made and good builders for the 4-point gap if black dances (fails to re-enter off the bar); in total there are 16 rolls that will fill the gap, one roll that will make the 1-point, and 13 that will hit the blot on white's 13-point; making a grand total of 30 working rolls out of 36!

Chan (w) : 4 Bensley (b) : 3

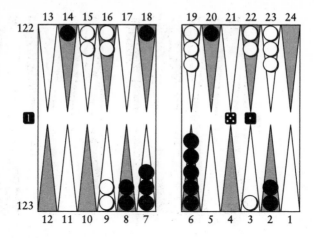

Figure 10.15

Black to play 5–1

51: 8/3* 3/2 (Snowie's position 3)
Black's **pick-and-pass** move of 8/3* 3/2 is just an annoyance to white and, with nothing else for black to pick up, all it does is clear a good point, the 8-point. Making the mid-point, 18/13 14/13 (which is a good blocking point as well as a safe haven for the runners) is by far the better play.

Ask yourself, 'Can I make a point?' If the answer is yes and it's a good point, make it! What you don't want to be doing is clearing off good points just for the sake of hitting. It could be argued that hitting in this position could assist the three (now four) black blots to get to safety – but it would be a spurious argument. White is very flat and unless he can escape his runner he'll be losing one of his points very soon.

Chan (w): 5 Bensley (b) : 3

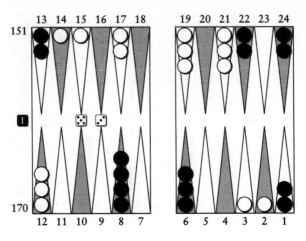

Figure 10.16

White to play 5–3

53: 11/6 13/10 (Snowie's position 2)
The actual play 11/6 13/10 is a missed opportunity to make the golden point, as Paul Magriel calls it; the 5-point. OK, making the 5-point leaves a return shot with 5s and 6–1, but remember this: once you've made your 5-point you almost never clear it until the bear-off – it becomes a fixed point and is well worth the risk in this instance. Does white really care if black breaks off the 22-point anchor to hit? Of course not.

Paul Magriel knows what he's talking about. More often than not, make the 5-point if you can – especially when your opponent has a very poor home board. The 5-point is the most important point on the board – you should make it whenever you get the chance unless in doing so you have to give up something better.

Chan (w) : 5 Bensley (b) : 3

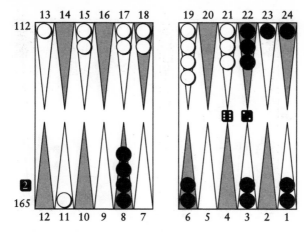

Figure 10.17

Black to play 6–2

62: 8/2 8/6 (Snowie's position 5)
Slotting the 2-point here by playing 8/2 is of no use, even if it does help clear a heavy point. The next points to make are the 5- and 4-points, in that order if possible. The 2 played 8/6 is correct. Shift the spare checker off the 22-point with the 6, 22/16. If it gets hit back you have a good chance of making another anchor.

Try to make your home-board points in descending order from the 6-point. Fill any gaps as soon as you can. In the position above, black does not want the 2-point, she wants the 5- or 4-point and to get her runners running. Running out to the 22-point certainly puts the blot 'under the gun', but with four points open re-entry shouldn't be a problem – 22 rolls (61.11 per cent) will get you off the bar.

Chan (w) : 7 Bensley (b) : 3

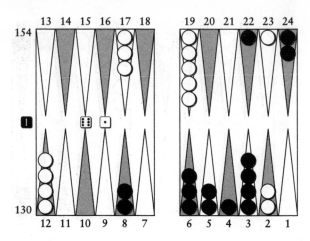

Figure 10.18

White to play 6–1

61: 8/2 13/12 (Snowie's position 3)
Do *not* make the 2-point. It is of no use to you at all, it would be better if the blot there was recirculated and put back into the game. The best move here should be obvious – make the bar–point, 13/7 8/7. At the moment black is struggling to get her runners out, so make it more difficult for her to do so by making the bar-point and forming a 3-prime.

Ask yourself, 'Can I make a point?' Well, in this instance you can make two; but the 2-point is far too deep and white should be concentrating on keeping the black runners in his home board. By making his bar-point, white is cutting down black's direct escaping rolls and could even force her to break off her 8-point.

Chan (w) : 7   Bensley (b) : 3

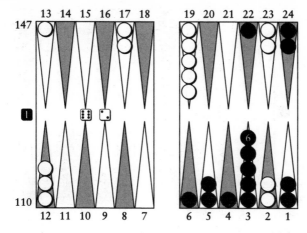

Figure 10.19

White to play 6–2

62: 12/6 23/21* (Snowie's position 3)
It is quite obvious that the 2 is played 23/21*; but what about
the 6? Well, the last place you want to put it is on the 6-point, on
top of the other five checkers! The best 6 is to move the back
checker 23/17 and prepare to repel the last four black checkers
as they scramble for home. Black's home board is crunching
nicely – and white has to make another point at least before he
becomes any sort of a threat.

*Don't stack on points that are already fully laden. Keep your
checkers well distributed. The most checkers you really need on
any one point is four, to use doubles when rolled; however, more
often than not three is enough. Try to distribute your checkers
evenly over the board to make maximum use of the 36 dice rolls.*

Chan (w) : 7 Bensley (b) : 3

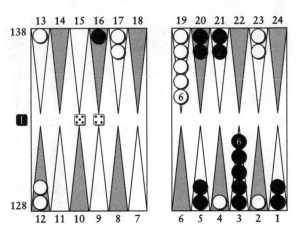

Figure 10.20

White to play 5–4

54: 13/8 13/9* (Snowie's position 7)
White plays an unnecessary hit and once again stacks on top of an existing point. Hitting here will not make much difference to black; the two-point board doesn't pose much of a threat. All white needs to do is be patient and try to attack in his home board. Playing 21/12 and covering the mid-point blot is excellent. If white thinks he'll get a hit in black's home board he's mistaken – while black has five checkers to move elsewhere, she won't be moving any at home. The white checker left behind on the 23-point is quite safe – and a big nuisance!

Recognize where the battle will be engaged. Hitting here is not a realistic ploy – in this position it is very wrong. It is important that white is ready to knock back any black blots he can, and at the same time he's got to keep the pressure on black – making the mid-point does this very well indeed.

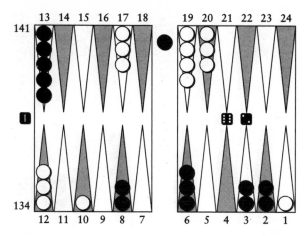

Figure 10.21

Black to play 6–2

62: 25/23 8/2 (Snowie's position 2)
What do you do with the 6? Well, playing 8/2 is a waste of a move and gains nothing if the blot is hit. It is far better here to slot the bar-point, 13/7 and if this is missed then there are excellent chances to make it next roll. Even if the blot is hit it can become useful in making an anchor.

Don't waste a roll by being afraid of being hit. Look at the opponent's home board and assess the risk first and your potential gain. Here the gain is enormous – the possibility to block off the black runner's direct escape. At the very worst black could be hit – and then she'd have the chance to make an anchor.

Coming in at Snowie's 2nd position might seem OK, but not when there are only three moves you can actually play!

Chan (w) : 10 Bensley (b) : 3

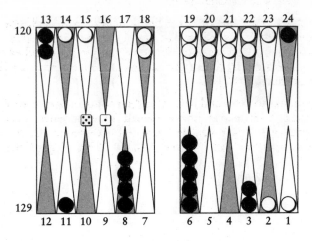

Figure 10.22

Crawford game, White to play 5–1

51: 10/4 (Snowie's position 8)

Black is doing badly in this game, the Crawford game. With the match to 11 points and the score at 10:3 to white, black needs to win to stay in the match. Moving 10/4 isn't a bad move, although it does come out at Snowie's position 8. If black rolls a 1 she's going to hit the blot, so getting your hit in first with 2/1* won't make any difference to that. If she does re-enter on a 1, her two-point board is nothing to fear and she'll still need another 1 to have any chance of escaping the prime. The 5 is moved 11/6 to cover the 1-point blot. If she re-enters with a 6–2 and runs out you'll have plenty of shots at the blot later on.

Sometimes, when you are hit with a roll no matter what you do, it is a good idea to consider hitting first. The odds of re-entry and escaping white's 5-prime are vastly against black.

This being the Crawford game (white is one point away from winning the match), gammons and backgammons aren't worth anything to him; however, the odds of white getting a gammon increase from 67.6 per cent with 10/4 to 74.2 per cent with the better move. Backgammon chances also increase from 31 per cent to 42 per cent.

Peter (white) went on to win the game and the match and became the 2003 Scottish Champion.

So, this was a game of errors and blunders from each side. It is hoped that this analysis will be of use in explaining the whys and wherefores of correct play. Often we analyse the matches of the top players and try to learn from their example; here we can learn just as much.

My thanks to Peter and Rosey for their contribution towards this chapter. Both players have gained in experience since this encounter – Rosey has had several successes in international tournaments and Peter played in the 2005 Las Vegas Open.

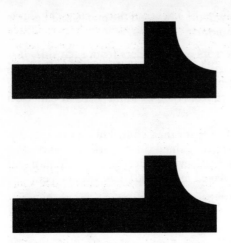

variations

In this chapter you will learn:

- about several variations, regional and 'occupational', of backgammon.

There are several variations of backgammon – regional variations and 'occupational' variations. I only deal with three in this book but there are many more. The three I have chosen are all different from each other and are the most well known of the variants. However, before I get to those let's take a look at a variation of modern backgammon in which more than two players can take part.

Chouette

Chouettes are played for money and, because of the numbers of players involved and the value of the doubling cube, huge sums of money can be won or lost – my advice to anyone considering playing in a chouette is to be very careful with whom you play and be certain you fully understand the rules played to. The actual game is no different from a simple head-to-head game between two players; what is different are some of the rules and the manner in which the doubling cube can be used. In chouette there is no one set of 'rules' except those that all players agree to before the start of play. I shall relate the rules to which my own club plays – others have their own set of 'rules'.

Any number of players can play in a chouette but it is better to keep to a reasonable number; in my example there are five players involved. To start, all players roll the dice and the player who rolls the highest number becomes the **box**, and the second highest, the **captain**; the remaining three players are graded in a similar order to produce an 'order of play' and they are the captain's team.

The box sits on one side of the board and the captain sits opposite him with the remaining players. The box is effectively playing against the other four players headed by their Captain. The game is essentially between the box and the captain, but the captain can be advised on his moves by the rest of his team. If the box loses the game he will lose four times the stake at whatever value the doubling cube is on. If the stake was £1 and he lost a gammon on a 2-cube, he would lose 4 × cube value × 2 = £16.

In some chouettes, automatic cubes are allowed – if the opening rolls of the box and captain are a double then the cube starts on 2 instead of on 1; and on the next roll the cube can be increased to 4 should another double be rolled. Some chouettes limit 'autos' to just one, some set no limit and others don't allow 'autos'; it all depends on the local rules in play at the time.

Team members can advise their captain at any time in some chouettes and in others they are not allowed to make any comments until their own doubling cube is in play. Players have their own cube and it can be offered at any time prior to the captain rolling. If the box refuses the cube offered he loses £1 and the 'winning' player sits out until this game is over. If the box accepts the doubling cube then that player is now playing for double the stakes, which is £2.

In most chouettes one rule is nearly always used, the Jacoby rule; a rule generally used in money play which disallows gammons and backgammons unless either player or side has accepted a double during the game. The benefit of this rule in a chouette is that it stops players playing on for un-doubled gammons or backgammons, thus speeding up the rate of play.

How the box actually loses a game, and therefore his position as box, is complicated. In my own club they have to show a profit to remain the box. For example, if they won £4 and lost £4 they would lose the box and go to the bottom of the team, and the captain would then become the new box and the next player in line would become the new captain. Others say the box is lost if the captain wins regardless of the profit.

Chouettes can be fun, especially when played with friends and for small stakes. Some high-rollers play for £10 a point and can win and lose thousands of pounds; just be absolutely certain you are aware of the stake and the 'rules' before joining in. If you can't afford to join, watch. You can learn a lot from watching and listening to the different arguments over the merits of Play A over Play B or Play C. In a chouette there can be as many 'best moves' as there are team members, each trying to convince their peers that theirs is the better one. Ultimately the captain will decide what move to make or what advice to heed or ignore – and his say is final.

Acey-duecy

A game popular with US Navy personnel **acey-duecy,** refers to a roll of 1–2 (ace and deuce), a throw that gives the player extra turns. Both sides start off with all 15 checkers *off* the board and the object is to get them all *on* the board and around and to bear them off as in conventional backgammon. Each player goes around in opposing directions starting from their opponent's home board.

The game gets exciting when 2–1 is rolled. This is played in the normal way and then, as a bonus, the player is allowed to *name any roll of doubles* and to play them; and then they roll again. If the subsequent roll is 2–1 the process is repeated until such time as a roll other than 2–1 is rolled or a roll of 2–1 cannot be fully played. As you will have gathered, luck plays a significant role in acey-duecy!

Plakoto

It's all Greek in this game played in the cafés and bars of Athens. Both players start with all 15 checkers on their 24-point; they travel in opposing directions and the first to bear all their checkers off is the winner.

The big difference with Plakoto is that instead of being placed on the bar when hit, blots are trapped by an opponent's checker and cannot move until released. The last checker to move from the 24-point is called the *mother*, and if it is trapped on the 24-point before it has moved the game is lost and you lose two points.

Tavla

The Turkish take delight at playing this variation of backgammon and it starts from a most startling position, as shown in figure 11.1.

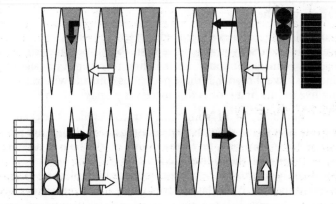

Figure 11.1

The two checkers at the start cannot be moved until the remaining 13 checkers are on the board. Checkers are entered as they are in conventional backgammon but with one difference, they cannot be entered upon a point occupied by any other checker, including your own; however, an opponent's blot can be landed upon and is placed on the bar.

Tavla is so dissimilar to modern backgammon that to fully explain its moves and rules would take a book in itself. However, 'modern' backgammon is also played in Turkey with subtle differences, and is also called tavla (which is confusing!). Here's an account of my experiences of playing in Turkey over the last 20 years.

Tavla is played everywhere in Turkey – shops, cafés, restaurants, bars, lokantas, hotels, pensions, pavements, even in the middle of the road! Entire sections of cities are pedestrianized solely for the pursuit and pleasure of playing tavla – or so it seems.

I refer to its Turkish name because, although it is the same backgammon that we all know and love, there are a few small variations in the way in which it is played. To my knowledge (and when it comes to playing tavla in Turkey that knowledge is widespread and hard gained) these rules or variations are not written down but are learnt as the game progresses!

Tavla is often played in the middle of the pavement and is frequently disturbed by uncaring and unsympathetic passers-by! These interruptions are essential to the full enjoyment of the game – I suspect even part of the rules – as they are an occasion for colourful invective questioning of the parentage and mental capacity of the perpetrators.

Normally the matches are played first to five points, best of three. Unless, of course, you reach five first, then it becomes clear that you have misunderstood and it is first to seven. Hindsight and analysis have shown that these occasions coincide with me reaching five points first – or is this merely my imagination?

The equipment is of some interest to regular backgammon players (not to mention distress) inasmuch as the dice are microscopic (as in tiny, tiny, tiny), the points on the boards are all the same colour (if they have a colour at all) and invariably the checkers appear to be the same colour for both players! Happily, closer inspection of the latter reveals that in fact one set of checkers is a different shade or has in some way been smudged to differentiate them from the opponent's.

This inspection continues throughout the match as you sit hunchbacked above the board staring myopically at each move. Finally, the board is placed upon a small, wobbly plastic table, which in turn is placed upon a rough and uneven surface giving the whole ensemble a nautical bent as the whole structure reels from side to side as though one were on board the ferry as Charon steers it drunkenly across the Styx. In fact, at the right (or wrong) time of year, the sun is so hot you might well believe you are actually nearing Hades.

I'd like to describe the dice in more detail. If you're the sort of player who only plays with precision dice, beware! Each die face is different from its five neighbours and the 1 is a large, round indentation, usually painted bright red. The fact that this large 'moon crater' of a dent might, just slightly, bias the fall of the die should not alarm the purists among you – this supposed bias is more than compensated for by the fact that Turkish dice are not formed of right-angles, thus ensuring a fair roll! However, there's fair and there's fair, as you will learn later.

So, the board is set, you've figured out which checkers are yours (the starting positions are a great help), you've narrowed your eyes to slits, better able to focus on the dice, you're crouched over the reeling board and the game begins.

You win the first throw, which establishes that you have the first move. You cup the dice in your hands (no dice cups here – the Turks don't hold with that sissy stuff, they're hands-on men) and you shake them ineffectively in your palms. Ineffectively because the occasion, the onlookers, the searing heat all conspire to make you perspire, even your palms sweat and the dice cling like limpets to your skin. Aha! You think you've learnt the reason why the Turks hold the dice between the first two fingers and the thumb. Wrong! Look again; they're not sweating, they hold them like that so they can roll the numbers they want! Oh yes they can – I told you earlier, there's fair and there's fair!

Anyway, you think you've sussed out how to hold the dice and you toss them on to the board. Now before we go any further let's just clarify a legal roll. As long as no die falls on to the road it is legal. They might be in separate tables, they might be on the checkers – it doesn't matter, it's legal.

So, back to your roll. The dice launch themselves from your grip, bounce on the board and, at the very moment they come to a halt your opponent's hand swoops down like some avenging angel, picks them up, rolls again and completes his move before your narrowed eyes have even had time to focus upon where yours fell, let alone upon what they fell.

The Turks don't mess about when playing tavla, oh no. It's played at a lightning pace – well, at least their move is. If you blink, cough, sneeze or turn your head for a second you'll miss half the game! Their half! They sneer at our slow play, they think we are women (for those readers that are women, they just think you're slow), and I can tell you, in a male-dominated society, your masculinity cannot withstand too many threats. The pace at which they play is incredible. Visually it's a blur, but aurally (and here's a major clue to knowing when they have actually moved) the loud 'crrrack' the checker makes as it's slapped to the board gives a directional clue as to the pieces moved.

Now, it's at this time that an optical illusion takes place as the checker is forced down, the table legs (wobbly plastic) buckle and the board is compressed to the ground; but the checkers appear to be suspended in midair, defying gravity. In reality they are awaiting the return of the board to its original position. Until one gets used to this phenomenon it's quite unnerving.

'Er, sorry, I didn't quite see what my throw was.' This is the stock phrase of the visiting tavla player and is closely followed by the much used, 'What is that in English?'

So you make your move. Whatever it is – good or bad – it will be sneered at. You can be certain of two things when making your play:

- making points is futile; your opponent will simply leap over all but a 6-prime with a convenient double.
- all blots will be hit. Yes, I know, you have to leave blots/builders, but I do assure you, if they're within the range of the dice, then unerringly, like some laser-guided bird of prey, your opponent will swoop down on your checker and, with a loud wallop, deposit it on the bar with a look that says, 'Why did you leave that?'

The ease and contempt with which Turkish players throw 6–6 consecutively to bear off is a revelation and a lesson in humility. All over Turkey you can hear the hissing of deflated egos. In fact, the scale of this deflation has been ascribed by certain meteorologists as the true source of the Sirocco and not the deserts of Libya as popularly thought.

So, there you have it. Backgammon in Turkey. I know I might have given you a couple of the rules but there is still more to learn. After 20 years I'm still learning.

I can thoroughly recommend playing tavla in Turkey. You will undoubtedly enjoy every minute of it, playing opposite the friendliest and most hospitable people you could ever wish to meet. All that's left is for me to figure out a way to beat my Turkish 'brother', Mustafa!

12

etiquette and tournament procedures

In this chapter you will learn:

- the etiquette a considerate backgammon player is expected to demonstrate towards his opponent
- how and why chess clocks are used in some tournaments.

Backgammon is a face-to-face game and the considerate backgammon player should practise good etiquette towards his opponent. Although most of what you are about to learn is related to tournament play it is also applicable when playing at home or elsewhere. Good manners and a sporting attitude will always ensure you're welcome back to play another time – even if you did beat your opponent!

Taking part in a tournament

Be sure to arrive at the tournament before the close of registration, and be certain to be in the playing room during the draw. When you hear your name called out, raise your hand to help your opponent identify you. When you are paired with an opponent, quietly move to a playing table and await the start of the tournament.

Before playing a game or match, ensure that the board is set up properly and that the cube (if used) is centred on the board between the two players. An incorrect checker starting position must be corrected prior to the fifth roll of the game. The set-up thereafter becomes official. Players starting with fewer than 15 checkers can still be gammoned or backgammoned.

Shake your opponent's hand and wish them a good game or match; this also applies at the end of a match when the score reaches DMP (double match point) and the outcome of this game will produce a winner.

Breaks are allowed between games and after matches; however, don't take too long over either or you could incur penalty points for being late. You will be expected to take a break at the same time as your opponent as only a certain number of breaks are allowed.

Each player should keep a running match score and compare it with their opponent's at the start of each game. This must clearly show each point won and clearly be displayed for the opponent to check and verify after each game, and for the Tournament Director to see on his trawls through the playing room. Some players use a 'score-board', a flip-over device that displays the score for all to see, but it must not replace a pen and paper record.

Playing a game

Shake your dice vigorously, using an up-and-down and side-to-side motion to ensure the dice are well shaken before rolling them simultaneously to the right of the bar. They should be thrown from a discernible height and be seen to bounce and roll freely across the board. If any dice are projected off the board and subsequently land back on the board then the entire roll will be deemed invalid and both dice must be rolled gain. Both dice must come to rest flat (not cocked) on the playing surface to the right of the bar; otherwise they must be rolled again. Under no circumstances should you roll your dice into the table to your left when playing in a tournament (or a serious game) because to do so could deem your roll invalid at your opponent's discretion. Sometimes players request permission from their opponents to roll in the outer board, especially during the bear-off when the home boards are full, which in a friendly game is fine but in a tournament I would strongly advise against it for it can lead to disputes.

You should move clearly, using only one hand to play the checkers. No player should move any checkers during an opponent's turn. You conclude your move by picking up your dice. Once your dice are picked up your move is ended and none of your checkers can be moved except at your opponent's discretion following an illegal move on your part. Upon drawing attention to an illegal move, your opponent may condone it or demand that the full roll be played legally. An illegal move is condoned by your opponent rolling their own dice or by turning the cube, thus starting his turn.

Wait until your opponent has picked up his dice before rolling your own. All premature actions (dice rolls or cube action), will stand if otherwise valid. An opponent who has yet to complete their turn or act upon the cube may then do so with the foreknowledge of your dice throw or cube action. This is a rule used by many Tournament Directors around the world and it is one to be very wary of – do not roll too soon and let your opponent change their mind after seeing your next roll.

You may only double when it is your turn to roll and you must do so before rolling (cocked dice are deemed 'rolling' dice). To offer a double or redouble, move the cube towards your opponent at the higher level, saying clearly, 'double' or similar. To take, draw the cube towards yourself and say, 'take' or similar, placing the cube on your side of the board. Both players should ensure that the correct level is displayed. To reject the cube one says, 'pass' or 'drop' and the game is concluded. Care should be exercised when handling the cube, as either verbal or physical acts might be interpreted as cube actions by an opponent.

When a player reaches match point, the Crawford rule will come into operation. This means the cube cannot be used by either player for that one game and should be removed from the board for this one game only. It should be returned to the board in the next game if the leader fails to win the game during the Crawford rule.

It is considered bad manners to call your opponent's bad rolls, or to laugh at their bad luck (although you can laugh *with* them as in the hard luck tale in Chapter 5).

Don't use a mobile phone or headphones while playing. Try to avoid conversations with third parties that might distract you or your opponent.

When the match or game is over, shake your opponent's hand and, if you are the loser, congratulate them on a their victory. Do not gloat or boast if you are the victor – shake hands and say, thanks for the game or something similar.

Finally, do not play too slowly. Backgammon is best played at a good pace. Playing too slowly can be very irritating for your opponent and can be quite disruptive during a tournament. As a beginner, you won't be expected to play all your moves swiftly but there will be many moves that you should be able to play without taking too much time over them. Try to get into the habit of knowing what rolls you want before rolling the dice. For example, if your opponent leaves you a blot seven pips away that you'd like to hit, and all combinations of 7 aren't much use anywhere else, don't look for a better play if you roll 6–1, 5–2 or 4–3 – just hit it!

Try to remain courteous at all times and treat your opponents as you'd like them to treat you.

Many of the rules in tournament play are interpreted by the Tournament Director. The rules and procedures are there to ensure fair play and not for the benefit of one player over another. If unsure about a ruling your opponent says is 'correct', call the Tournament Director over for clarification.

Clocks in backgammon

Many players these days are taking longer and longer to play their matches. This causes delays during tournaments and has led in many areas to the use of the chess clock as a timekeeper. Personally I don't like the use of chess clocks in backgammon and I try to avoid their use as often as I can. Unfortunately, the slower players are increasing in number and clocks are being used with greater frequency.

Tournament Directors usually allow between five and seven minutes per game when applying clocks. Under Biba Clock Rules the Director will place 12 seconds per move on each player's clock, plus a reserve of two minutes for each point needed to complete a new match. The reserve time is only used when a player exceeds 12 seconds per move. For matches already started the reserve will be reduced by one minute for every point scored by both players.

When a player's time reserve is exhausted he has lost the match unless it is at match point (or similar[1]) and in a position where it is mathematically impossible for an opponent to win or save a gammon or backgammon, thus saving the match.

Before playing with clocks, first check the clock rules and familiarize yourself with them. Often such knowledge can mean the difference between winning and losing.

Playing with clocks is somewhat different from playing without them. With clocks in use only one set of dice is used and they are shared by both players. After shaking and rolling his dice a player moves his checkers and concludes his move by pushing down his clock button, with the same hand used to make the move, to start their opponent's clock. The opponent then picks up the dice (or cube if he wants to double the stakes) and repeats the whole process.

Both clocks are stopped only for the following reasons:

- to start a new game
- to offer a concession

---

1. Gammons and backgammons, where possible, will count (× cube value) for players at a score that, such points won, would win them the match.

2. Prior to each break both players must record the clock times on the score card. This action is designed to prohibit players or third parties from altering the time lapsed.

- to announce an intention to take an authorized break in the match[2]
- to retrieve fallen dice
- to contest an opponent's action
- to summon the Director.

Playing with chess clocks can be very distracting and many players dislike them immensely. If you'd like to avoid using clocks, my advice is to play at a decent pace and only slow right down when considering awkward rolls or cube decisions. I have seen many finals decided on timing rather than on checker-play, and that includes the finals of World Championship matches!

13

the history of backgammon

In this chapter you will learn:

- that backgammon is an ancient game
- how different games from different cultures have contributed to the game of today
- about more recent developments in the game.

Backgammon has had a long and sometimes turbulent history, at times courted by kings, at times banned by kings! Always popular, always exciting, always unpredictable, it has evolved over the centuries to become one of the most popular board games in the world.

Ancient history

Backgammon is also considered to be the oldest board game in the world, even older than chess. An early version of what is now believed to be an ancestor of backgammon was first played about 5,000 years ago by the Sumerians, in southern Mesopotamia, today's modern Iraq. This is known because British archaeologist, Sir Charles Leonard Woolley, in the city of Ur in the 1920s, unearthed an early game board. Five thousand years ago Ur was on the Persian Gulf, but its location now is much further inland and is named Tell el-Mukayyar, situated south of Baghdad. During Saddam Hussein's rule a miltary complex was stationed close by and the site was closed down. It remains closed to my knowledge.

The chamber in which the board was found had been broken into centuries earlier by grave robbers and all that remained were two model boats and the 'backgammon' board. The board was an ornate, inlaid one and not like the boards we recognize today as backgammon boards. Not long after Woolley's discovery, archaeologists discovered another gaming board in another part of Mesopotamia. Not as elaborate as the first one, it was found complete with two sets of 'checkers' and 'dice', making a close link to today's components of the game.

I find it fascinating that in addition to 'inventing' backgammon, the Sumerians were the first civilization to develop a written language. It was *cuneiform*, or wedge-shaped, and we all know what popular board game is played on a board consisting of 24 wedge-shaped 'points', don't we?

As 'recently' as 1500 BC, Egyptian pharaohs were playing *senet*, another board game that appears to resemble backgammon. One very famous board was discovered in Tutankhamen's tomb. Queen Nefertari is seen playing senet in wall paintings in the tombs. Although senet was based on a board with 30 squares, the shape they formed are very unlike the backgammon boards of today. Senet boards were placed in tombs as a kind of good-luck charm for the journey into the afterlife. Successful senet players were thought to be favoured by the gods – a belief founded perhaps on the luck element of the game. So popular was senet that it is even mentioned in the *Book of the Dead*.

Next we travel to India where *pachisi*, another backgammon ancestor, appears to have originated. Pachisi was a four-player game played with six or seven cowrie shells (such shells were used as dice); but it did share many similarities with backgammon as we know it today: it was a race-game; rolling certain cowrie combinations allowed a player to take an extra roll; the object was to be the first player to get all four of their checkers around the board and home; checkers could be hit and taken off the board; some checker positions were so strong that opponent's checkers could not pass them. These similarities with the modern game make pachisi a contributory ancestor even though the board design was that of a symmetrical cross.

The Greeks played a form of the game that is mentioned several times by Greek philosophers and scholars. Plato and Sophocles both make references to it and most probably played the game themselves.

To find a more recognizable version we move to Rome in the first century AD. Here we find *ludus duodecim scriptorum* or *XII Scripta*, so named for the 12 points on either side of the board. One big difference between *ludus duodecim scriptorum* and backgammon is that *ludus duodecim scriptorum* used three dice instead of two. The Romans took their 'game of 12' very seriously. The Emperor Claudius was reputed to have written a book on the game; Marc Antony and Cleopatra are thought to have idled away the hours playing it. Two Emperors, Nero and Commodus, were supposedly so smitten by the gambling aspect of what was becoming known by its more popular name, *tabula* (board), that they wagered, and lost, huge sums of money playing it.

It wasn't just Emperors who were addicted to the game and gambling, ordinary Romans were also setting wagers on the game. At Pompeii two wall paintings show scenes of *tabula* being played – in one, two players are seen arguing over a game being played and in the other an inn-keeper is seen throwing the players out into the street.

It was the Romans who brought *tabula*, or 'tables' as it became known in Britain, to Europe. In 480 AD Emperor Zeno was the victim of some unlucky dice (three of them!) when he rolled a 2,

5 and 6. He had to break his blocking points and he lost the game. It would appear that *tabula* was almost identical to modern backgammon except in one very significant respect – it used three dice.

It would appear that the Romans were worried about dice-rigging, or dice-mechanics, for it was they that introduced the dice-box; a device for producing random rolls of the dice. Even today dice-boxes are in use and occasionally make an appearance at international tournaments.

More recent history

It wasn't until the twelfth century and the Crusades that tables gained in popularity, but in a slightly altered form. For many years *nard* had been played in the Middle East, originating in Persia (modern Iran) and it was this variation that the Crusaders brought back with them on their return. This version of tables was played using two dice on a board identical to a modern backgammon board and is reckoned by many to be the true beginning of backgammon as we know it today. It is possible that the variation, *Irish*, was in fact this version. Irish was very popular throughout Europe, and it had many names.

The *Game of Kings* became the game of soldiers. Playing tables was so popular that Richard the Lionheart and Philip of France issued a joint act banning it and other gambling games in 1190; however, Richard and his brother, John were not precluded from playing! In 1841, historian Joseph Strutt informs us that the decree passed by Richard I not only prohibited any person in the army beneath the rank of a knight from playing any sort of game for money, but that none of them was permitted to lose more than 20 shillings in one day. To lose more would incur a penalty of 100 shillings. Of course, both Richard and Philip were under no such restrictions, but their attendants were restricted to the same amount as the knights (20 shillings) and their penalty for losing more was to be whipped naked for three days.

Cardinal Wolsey decreed the game, along with dice, cards and bowls, illegal in 1526 and ordered that all gaming boards were to be burned. It is this act that is thought to have given birth to the folding backgammon board that is so common today. Backgammon boards were disguised as books and could be folded away and hidden among the books on library shelves and in cupboards. It attained the status of *inhonesti ludi*, 'dishonest games', and the Catholic Church waged war against it. (Saint) Louis IX of France extended the ban to his subjects and court officials. Tables was suppressed (as far as was possible – but with little success) until the end of the fifteenth century.

One of the most famous backgammon boards of this time was discovered on Henry VIII's flagship, *The Mary Rose*, which sank in Plymouth harbour in 1545. Discovered in a chest in the carpenter's cabin, the board is exactly as we play upon today. It was recovered complete with bone dice and wooden checkers. After the ship was raised in 1982 the board was placed in the *Mary Rose* Museum in Plymouth. In 1996 the Director of Special Events of the Hilton hotel chain, Stuart Jackson, and Michael Crane, the Director of the British Isles Backgammon Association, commissioned a replica of the board. Built by master-craftsman Chris Woolcott of Lincoln, it was constructed using the same woods and techniques as used by its original creator. The board is now owned by Nicky Check who won it at the 1997 *Mary Rose* backgammon tournament. It is a unique board and an object of beauty and craftsmanship.

Another famous backgammon set was the Gloucester Tables Set, excavated in 1983 and reputed to have been owned by William Rufus. Each of the checkers has been carved with Romanesque images. The checkers, all made from bone, are mostly well preserved and depict several themes: good and evil, the zodiac, natural history, the calendar and Biblical references. The board is on display in the Gloucester City Museum along with its checkers.

Throughout the centuries many authors and scholars have written about backgammon: Shakespeare in *Love's Labours Lost*; Thackery in *Vanity Fair*; Douglas William Jerrold is quoted as saying, 'The only athletic sport I ever mastered was backgammon'; Sir Arthur Conan-Doyle in the Sherlock Holmes story, *The Five Orange Pips*; Chaucer in *The Canterbury Tales*; Spenser in *The Faerie Queene*; Samuel Pepys in his diaries; Lord Byron wrote in *Don Juan*: 'Like a backgammon board, the place was dotted with whites and blacks'; The Roman poet, Ovid is said to make a reference to *ludus duodecim scriptorum* in his *Ars Amatoria* ('The Art of Love'), which, being a 'sex manual', puts backgammon in a whole new light!

The most famous, perhaps, is *Hoyles Treatise on the game of Back-Gammon* [sic] in 1743 by Edward Hoyle. In 1745 he codified the 'rules' of backgammon and to the present day many of these rules still apply, albeit slightly altered after being modified in 1931 in America.

However, the word 'backgammon' was perhaps first used in the mid-seventeenth century. It was here that the old and new appear to meet. Games historian, H.J.R. Murray, in *A History of Board Games Other Than Chess*, originally published in 1801, informs us that the differences between *tables* and backgammon are that in backgammon doublets are played twice and that a 'backgammon' is worth three points. This is still applicable today.

Modern backgammon

We now arrive at what we understand as backgammon. There is some speculation as to where the actual name originated. It might be from the Welsh, *bach* (or bac), meaning small, and *cammaun* meaning battle to form 'little battle'. Or it could be from the Middle English, *baec*, which means back, and *gamen*, which means game to give us 'back game'. Or perhaps it was derived from the fact that many backgammon boards could be found on the reverse side of a chessboard. No-one knows for certain and therefore we are at liberty to choose our own favourite origin. According to the *Oxford Universal Dictionary*, the earliest recorded use of the word 'backgammon' was in 1645.

In France the game was known as *tric-trac*, perhaps so called because of the sound the checkers made when moved across the wooden boards and tables upon which the game was played. Louis XIII and Louis XVI each had specially designed tric-trac tables; such articles of furniture becoming very popular in the homes of the aristocracy, among them Marie Antoinette. Marie Antoinette lost her head in more ways than one for it is said that one tric-trac table cost her 238,000 francs in gold! During one game she is reputed to have lost deliberately to her opponent to pay off an embarrassing debt he had accrued. Its association with the aristocracy doomed tric-trac boards and tables to be destroyed during the Revolution.

For whatever reason, backgammon's popularity waned towards the end of the nineteenth century in Europe (although it remained popular with the gentry and affluent, the common man lost interest) and it is to America that we turn to see what caused its rebirth into the modern version we all play today. Although not as popular in the United States, it had been played there since the seventeenth century. Thomas Jefferson was a keen player and an ardent recorder of his gaming winnings and losses, details of which he kept in a notebook. It was the gambling side of backgammon that heralded its reincarnation.

Unfortunately, history doesn't record who invented the doubling cube, but it is known to be a player in America who came up with the idea of doubling the stakes throughout a game. This one idea revolutionized backgammon and it enjoyed a surge in popularity upon which it is still riding. Almost overnight backgammon became perhaps the most exciting gambling game there is.

For centuries backgammon and gambling have been closely linked – perhaps good reasons for its banning and punitive repercussions; but with the advent of gaming clubs in America, backgammon tournaments became popular. Soon, tournaments were being played all over the world. The World Championships were first held in 1967 in Las Vegas and were won by Tim Holland; they moved to the Bahamas in 1975 and then to Monte Carlo (their present home) in 1976–79 (there's a small overlap due to there being two world championships for a few years!). Now there's a backgammon tournament almost every day somewhere or other.

For a long time the Americans dominated the game. They began to lose their grip in the 1990s when European players such as Phillip Marmorstein (Germany) and Michael Meyburg (Germany) came to prominence. Latterly the Scandinavians have been doing very well, winning five of the last six world championships: 1999 and 2001 Jurgen Granstedt (Sweden), 2002 Mads Andersen (Denmark), 2003 Jon Røyset (Norway), 2004 Peter Hallberg (Denmark). However, in 2005 the Americans fought back and the winner was Dennis Carlston (USA), with fellow American, John O'Hagan the Runner-up. Europe prevailed in 2006 when Philip Vischjager (Netherlands) wrested the title back.

Soon, books on backgammon began to appear. Established players such as Paul Magriel started writing about the game and its strategies and tactics; his spartanly named, *Backgammon* being the one book all serious players have in their library. Although first published in 1976, much of its content is relevant today and it is an excellent book for players of all levels.

In the early 1990s Gerald Tesauro of IBM's Watson Research Center developed **TD-Gammon**, a backgammon-playing computer program. It was the first backgammon program that used artificial neural network technology. Playing 300,000 games against itself it learnt from the outcome to become so strong that Gerald challenged former World Champion, Bill Robertie to play against it in a 31-point match. The resultant book, *Learning from the Machine*, written by Robertie, became a backgammon bestseller.

An upsurge in playing ability was a direct result of the introduction of online backgammon servers and dedicated backgammon playing computer software such as JellyFish™ and Snowie™. The first online server was the aptly named, First Internet Backgammon Server (FIBS), which started in 1992. Now, in 2006, there are numerous sites on which to play – some very good and many very poor.

Backgammon in the UK had a surge of interest in the 1970s with the formation of The Backgammon Club of Great Britain. Sponsored by Phillip Morris, the tobacco company, it enjoyed a limited lifetime until the sponsor pulled out in the early 1980s. The now defunct National Backgammon Players Society of Great Britain (NBPS), of which your author was a founding member, ran from 1983 to its slow demise in the middle 1990s. In 1989 the British Isles Backgammon Association (Biba) was formed and is still going strong. Its continued commitment to backgammon has ensured that there's a healthy amount of backgammon being played throughout the UK in clubs run by Biba members.

There have been no major changes to how we play 'international' backgammon since the 1930s, except that the ability to analyse matches using software such as Snowie™ and Gnu has changed what plays we make with certain dice rolls. As yet there is no one set of rules that is played to worldwide; and none is on the horizon. As popular as backgammon is today, it has far to go to catch up with chess or bridge (or more recently poker, which has tens of thousands of players worldwide on the Internet) but, who knows what the future might hold? All it will take is another revolutionary idea like the doubling cube! Perhaps the $1 million tournament scheduled for the Bahamas in 2007 will be such an idea.

taking it further

This section lists places to play and software to help you improve your game, publications to read and study and books to pore over. There's a lot of backgammon out there just waiting for you to discover it. The Internet is perhaps the biggest source of backgammon information, but there's still a lot of 'real' backgammon action out there too.

Magazines

Bibafax is the subscription magazine of the British Isles Backgammon Association (Biba). Available in full colour, black and white or on CD-ROM, it features articles and quizzes alongside tournament reports and results. A free black and white copy or CD-ROM version can be obtained by contacting Biba via the website: www.backgammon-biba.co.uk.

Chicago Point is edited by Bill Davis and is aimed primarily at the USA; however, it does contain many articles and can be enjoyed by everyone. Many of its columnists are experts in their field and very respected among their peers (website: www.chicagopoint.com/index.html).

Flint Area Backgammon News is a publication based in Flint, Michigan, which might sound a little parochial but in fact it has a worldwide subscriber base and features many articles by world experts (website: www.flintbg.com/).

Make Your Point is the magazine of Gammonitis, a UK-based organization that hosts events for money players. A sample copy can be requested from them at www.gammonitis.com.

Books

There are a lot of books on the market that will take you to the heady heights of expert and advanced; however, there are few that start you off gently and take you by the hand through the technicalities. Many of them assume you have a sound basic knowledge of backgammon (you have read and understood the contents of this book!), without which you'll be floundering trying to understand a good deal of the content. Few books cater from beginner to intermediate/advanced, but three stand out: one a classic from 1976, one from 1993 by perhaps the best player in the world, and finally a modern approach from 2005. If you only buy one more book on backgammon, let it be one of these three – however, I recommend you add all three to your backgammon library.

- *Backgammon* by Paul Magriel. First published in 1976, 404 pages. Softcover reprint 1996.
  In the world of backgammon this much-respected book is known as the 'Bible'. Two years after publishing *Backgammon*, Paul won the 1978 World Championship in the Bahamas. He uses concise non-technical language, breaking down every aspect of backgammon so it's easy to understand even when discussing advanced theories of the game. *Backgammon* is the definitive backgammon book. It can turn a beginner into an expert. Well written, logically organized, with numerous diagrams and clear explanations, it is a must for any player!
- *Backgammon For Winners* by Bill Robertie. Paperback published 1993, 131 pages.
  Two-times World Champion (1983 and 1987) Bill Robertie is reckoned by many to be the best backgammon player in the world; this is just one of the many books written by him. Its content is impressive: more than 100 easy-to-understand diagrams; how to annotate a backgammon game; advanced backgammon play; powerful openings; dynamic and winning strategies; step-by-step explanations of all strategies; three sample games with move-by-move insights; Bill Robertie's inside secrets for dynamic winning play. Once you have read and mastered the content of this book, you'll be ready to take on Bill himself!
- *Backgammon Boot Camp* by Walter Trice. Paperback published 2005, 339 pages.
  Walter's book covers every aspect of the modern game, from the basics to advanced. Originally the book was a series of weekly articles on Gammon Village and it is written in a

'weekly' style to lead you deeper and deeper into the subtleties and nuances of the modern game. Whatever your level of expertise, this book will make a difference to your game. *Backgammon Boot Camp* will introduce you to concepts – and encourage you to think about backgammon in a way that will get you playing better, winning backgammon.

Merchandise

As you might have noticed, books and backgammon boards are quite rare in the high street stores. What you will find is limited in its choice and not always what you are looking for. The best sources of backgammon merchandise are to be found on the Internet. Three are recommended; one based in the UK, one in the USA and the other in Canada.

- Operated by Chris Ternel, Backgammon and Board Games Shop (www.bgshop.com) has an extensive range of backgammon-related merchandise including the books mentioned above. From dice to sets of checkers, Backgammon and Board Games Shop should have everything you desire. A selection of Chris's wares can be seen at most Biba tournaments, giving you an opportunity to see and touch and even play with/on any product you're considering obtaining.
- Carol Cole is a US-based shop via *Flint Area Backgammon News* (www.flintbg.com). Merchandise is shipped to the UK on a regular basis and Carol strives to keep costs as low as she can.
- If you can't find it at Backgammon and Board Games Shop then you'll find at *Gammon Village* (www.gammonvillage. com). It stocks a good selection of everything backgammon – books, boards, dice, aids.

Internet resources

- *Gammon Village* (www.gammonvillage.com) is an online magazine and well worth subscribing to. It does offer free viewing of some of its content but the good stuff is only available to members. It features articles from some of the top writers/players in the world in addition to tournament reports and match analysis. The majority of its content is for subscribers only, but non-subscribers can access a substantial number of its many articles. Subscriptions start from $20 for one month up to $50 for one year.

- Backgammon Galore (www.bkgm.com) – The name of this site says it all; there's almost everything you'll ever need to know on this website, and what cannot be found here will more than likely have a link to it elsewhere. Founded and edited by Tom Keith, it is one of the most popular and useful backgammon resources on the Internet.
- Gammon Links (www.chicagopoint.com/links.html) – This website from Mel Leifer has an extensive list of links to almost every backgammon related resource on the Internet. Mel is constantly updating it to keep on top of all new backgammon development. The database is sub-divided into ten categories making it easy to find whatever you're looking for.
- Mark Your Calendar (www.chicagopoint.com/calendar.html) – If you're looking to play tournament backgammon anywhere in the world then this site, edited by Carol Joy Cole (of *Flint Area BG News*) is the best place on the Internet to find it. Carol features every major (and some not so major) backgammon event there is, many with website links or email addresses for further information. It is updated very regularly and is divided into USA and Non-USA events.
- The Doubling Cube (www.thedoublingcube.com/index.htm) – This is a recent addition to online backgammon resources and I've mentioned it here because it is the brainchild of Jake Jacobs, a very respected backgammon expert and author. Don't be fooled by the site's name, it features a lot more than just cube information.
- *Gammonline* (www.gammonline.com) is an online backgammon magazine edited by Kit Woolsey, an undisputed expert on the game. It has many features: match of the month; a fully annotated match; quiz of the month; a set of difficult problems, analysed by a panel of experts (readers can send in their own answers, and the highest scoring answer set will win a prize); an ongoing match between Kit and the readers, with the readers' move chosen by a vote of the readers each day. There is a small charge made to access the content, but you can see a demo issue before you decide to subscribe. At the time of going to press the cost was $36 a year – a small price to pay for such a quality publication.

Online backgammon

There are hundreds of backgammon playing websites, some of which are very good, and some of which are not. Most, but not all, offer a ranking system, and many of them allow you to play for free. You also have the option to play for real money – or, in some cases, pretend money! Here are a few of the more popular sites, in alphabetical order.

- F.I.B.S., The First Internet Backgammon Server (www.fibs.com) started in 1992. As the name implies, FIBS is the oldest of the online backgammon servers and has been the training ground for many of the world's top players. It has a dedicated membership that work together to keep it running and updated.
- GamesGrid (www.gamesgrid.com), up and running in 1996, has a reputation for featuring many of the top players in the world. It appeared after FIBS and straight away attracted a cult following. Unlike FIBS, this server, and those that are mentioned below, have their own graphic interface.
- Gammon Empire (www.gammonempire.com) is one of the newer sites, formed in November 2004. It has a good-looking interface (one it shares with Play65 – see below) and is fast becoming one of the biggest sources of online backgammon at the moment.
- MSN Games (zone.msn.com/en/backgammon/), Microsoft's own backgammon player, started in 1997, is not as good as some of the competition, but plenty good enough to try out as a beginner.
- NetGammon (www.netgammon.com) arrived on the scene in 1996 and quickly gained in popularity with intermediate players and beginners. A little out of fashion with the very top players, it still attracts over 200,000 from over 150 countries.
- Play65 (www.play65.com) is another of the new ones from 2005. Play65 shares a lot in common with Gammon Empire: interface, banker, playing strength and numbers of players online at any one time. It is hard to tell them apart and preferring one to the other is, quite frankly, a matter of personal preference.
- PlaymakerWorld (www.playmakerworld.com), formed in 2001, soon became a leader in customization, allowing members to choose/design their own boards. A very popular site.
- TrueMoneygames (www.truemoneygames.com) started in 2002. As its name implies, this is the site to visit if you want to play for money. It has great sounds and graphics and is very popular with money players.
- *Yahoo*! (http://yahoo.com/games/) started in 1998 and caters for the casual player. It's one to cut your teeth on but not for the serious player.

Where to play

Depending upon where you live there is probably a backgammon club or an event near you. Head-to-head backgammon is far more fun than playing online. It's a social affair and enables players to meet, discuss and exchange views in a way the Internet never can. Two web-based sites below will inform you of what's happening and where; and the others are where, in the UK, beginners and improvers are welcome for modest fees; the last mentioned is aimed at money players

- **UK and European Clubs** – The web pages of BIBA (www. backgammon-biba.co.uk) have details of local and European clubs at www.backgammon-biba.co.uk/clubs.html and www. backgammon-biba.co.uk/EuropeanBGnews.htm. Also, the web page on how to form your own club (Local Club) is handy.
- **US Clubs** – There is a very comprehensive list of clubs in North America at www.chicagopoint.com/usaclubs.html.
- **British Isles Backgammon Association** – Formed in 1989 by Michael Crane, the association has been the leader in backgammon development and communication since its inception. Tournaments for all skill levels, from beginners to experts, are held every month and a ranking system enables all members to see exactly how they are progressing. Visit the website at www.backgammon-biba.co.uk.
- **Mind Sports Olympiad** – Backgammon is just one of dozens of games played at the Mind Sports Olympiad each August. Over a ten-day period backgammon players of all levels can take part in eight different events ranging from 1-point to 11-point matches – something to please any player of any level. It can be found at www.msoworld.com
- **Gammonitis** – This is a UK-based organization that caters for the more experienced player looking for money tournaments. Beginners are welcome but please bear in mind that the emphasis is on high stakes and, as such, top money players make up the bulk of entrants. It can be found at www.-gammonitis.com

Software

There's a plethora of software available to play against and learn how to play backgammon. Three of them stand out, one of which is totally free to use (Gnu) and two commercial programs (Snowie™ and JellyFish™).

Gnu

Gnu is totally free backgammon playing software released under the GNU General Public License. You can copy it and distribute among your friends if you wish. It is an 'open source' and is continually being improved and updated. A certain amount of computer literacy is required to download and install the software, but it is well worth doing. It features a handy interface that allows a graphical representation of the board to be displayed on your PC monitor.

Gnu plays at 2-ply lookahead (it looks ahead two moves) and despite the fact that it is totally free it plays as well (or better according to some) than its commercial rivals. Its rollouts are as good, if not better, than those of its costly rivals, and it is considered to be the best program available by many of its dedicated users. A copy can be downloaded from here: www.gnubg.org/

JellyFish™

The first commercially available backgammon playing program for the PC, JellyFish™ is the perfect starting tool for the beginner. It comes in three versions: Player, Tutor and Analyser. The Player version will only play backgammon, whereas the Tutor version will offer considerable help with identifying the best move and doubling decisions. The Analyser is the best option; it allows the user to roll out a position (play a position thousands of times) to establish the best move for any position. The board interface is very good with the option to change all the relevant colours.

Snowie™

Coming in the wake of JellyFish™, Snowie™ stormed ahead of its rival with a whole raft of features and playing ability. Without a doubt it is streets ahead of JellyFish™ and this is reflected in its cost; however, if money isn't an object then Snowie™ is the one to go for.

One of its main features is the analysis it carries out. The results are displayed in a user-friendly, user-controlled interface and give an instant graphical display of any errors or blunders in checker play or cube decisions. It is this facility that sets it apart from its rival and one of the features that will help you improve your game.

Both JellyFish™ and Snowie™ are available from the Biba Shop on the Biba website.

a test of knowledge

So, having read through the book this far, how much have you learnt about this fascinating and exciting game? After each question, write down your answer and then check at the end of this section to see how much you actually know.

Questions

1 What is an exposed or lone checker on a point called?
2 What point is referred to as the 'golden point'?
3 What moves would you make with these opening rolls?

   a) 4–2
   b) 6–1
   c) 3–1
   d) 6–5

4 From whose ship was a backgammon set recovered and what was the ship called?
5 What innovative addition to the modern game was introduced in the 1920s?
6 How many points does each player occupy at the start of a game?
7 What is the base number for calculating how many dice rolls will contain a certain number?
8 How many rolls out of 36 will enter a checker off the bar if three points are closed in an opponent's home board?
9 What does the acronym PRaT stand for?
10 When bearing off your last two checkers, place the following positions in descending order of the number of bearing-off rolls:

a) on the 6 and 1 points
b) on the 4 and 1 points
c) on the 5 and 2 points
d) on the 4 and 3 points

11 Generally, at what lowest (approximate) percentage chance of winning a game should you consider taking a double?

12 How many pips is a 6-prime block of two checkers per point in your home board?

13 Many players confuse slotting with splitting. Are the following statements correct?

  • Slotting – to separate two checkers that are together on a point.
  • Splitting – to play a single checker on to an empty point.

14 Playing in a chouette as the box against three other players, you win a gammon on a 2-cube. At £1 per point, how much money do you win?

15 How many opening rolls are there excluding doubles?

16 When playing with chess clocks there are certain times when you can legally stop both clocks. Look at the list below and see if you can find the two incorrect entries.

  a) to start a new game
  b) to retrieve fallen dice
  c) to consider a cube decision
  d) to announce an intention to take an authorized break in the match
  e) to do a pip-count
  f) to offer a concession
  g) to contest an opponent's action
  h) to summon the Director

17 You have four building points with enough checkers on to make another point. How many rolls out of 36 will make a point:
  a) excluding doubles?
  b) including doubles?

18 What is your 7-point better known as?

19 Prior to which roll must an incorrect checker starting position be corrected?

20 When was backgammon first played, and by whom?

21 What is the pip-count in this position shown in figure 1?

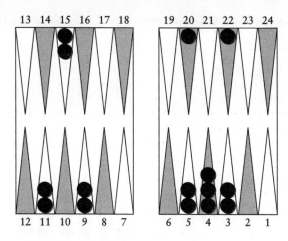

Figure 1

22 What is the pip-count in the position shown in figure 2

    a) for black?
    b) for white?

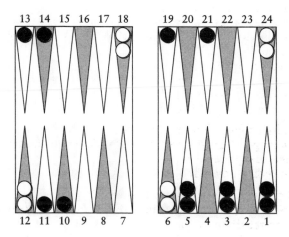

Figure 2

23 In figure 3, should black double to 2? Should white take if doubled?

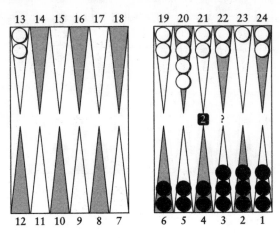

Figure 3

24 Black to play 3–1 in figure 4.

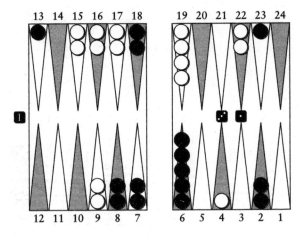

Figure 4

25 Black to play 3–2 in figure 5.

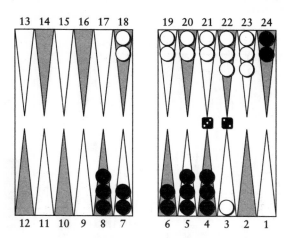

Figure 5

26 In figure 6, if white is on roll, who is favourite to win the game?

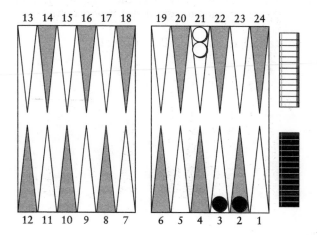

Figure 6

27 In figure 7, if black is on roll, should black recube to 8? Should white accept? The match is to seven points and black leads 2–1.

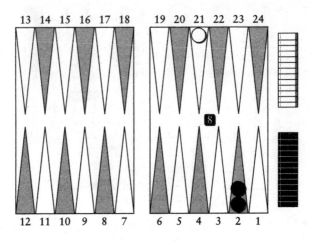

Figure 7

28 Under Biba Clock Rules, how many seconds per move and how many minutes reserve will the Director place on each player's clock needed to complete a new match?

29 What is a crossover?

30 Who wrote *Backgammon Boot Camp*?

Answers

1 An exposed or lone checker is called a blot.
2 The 20-point is referred to as the golden point.
3 The correct moves are:

   a) 4–2: make your 4-point by playing 6/4 2/4
   b) 6–1: make your bar-point by playing 13/7 8/7
   c) 3–1: make your 5-point by playing 8/5 6/5
   d) 6–5: move a back checker (runner) to your mid-point (13-point) 24/13

4 The set was recovered from Henry VIII's ship, *The Mary Rose*.
5 The doubling cube was introduced in the 1920s.
6 At the start of a game each player occupies four points.
7 Eleven is used as a base for calculating how many dice rolls will contain a certain number.
8 Seventy-five per cent of the rolls (27) will re-enter one checker off the bar against three closed points.
9 The acronym stands for Position, Race and Threat.
10 When bearing off your last two checkers the correct order is:

   b) 4 and 1 with 28 rolls
   c) 5 and 2 with 19 rolls
   d) 4 and 3 with 17 rolls
   a) 6 and 1 with 15 rolls

11 Generally you should consider taking a double with approximately 25 per cent chance.
12 A 6-prime block of two checkers per point in your home board is 42 pips.
13 The statement is incorrect, it should be:

   • Splitting – to separate two checkers that are together on a point.
   • Slotting – to play a single checker on to an empty point.

14 At £1 per point you would win £12; £4 from each opponent.
15 There are 30 opening rolls excluding doubles.
16 The two incorrect entries are:

   c) to consider a cube decision
   e) to do a pip-count.

17 Twelve rolls will make a point excluding doubles, and 16 will make a point including doubles.
18 Your 7-point is better known as your bar-point.

19 An incorrect checker starting position must be corrected prior to the fifth roll of the game.

20 Backgammon was first played about 5,000 years ago by the Sumerians.

21 The pip-count is 140.

22 a) 106
   b) 80

23 Black should double and white should drop.

24 Black should play 8/5, 6/5 and make the 5-point.

25 The best play for black is 8/3* giving white chances to break his home-prime.

26 Most players would look at white's bad rolls, 1s, 2s and 3s (not counting double 2s or 3s) and reckon that black is favourite, but they would be wrong. In this position, white is favourite with 51.3 per cent. Black will fail to clear with any roll of 1, and white is huge favourite to clear on the second roll if black rolls a 1.

27 Well it couldn't be closer – four pips each and black has only ten bad rolls, all 1s except double-1. This is a classic reference position and is paradoxically a redouble and a take. Black will win outright 72.2 per cent of the time; when he fails 27.8 per cent of the time white has to clear on one roll, and the only roll that won't do it for him is 2–1. Generally a player needs approximately 25 per cent to take, and white has 27.8 per cent. If black were to drop this cube then the score would shift to 1-away, 6-away, a position which leaves him just 10 per cent match-winning chances. It's a take!

   I recorded this position, which occurred at the 2000 World Cup Championships in Istanbul, during the doubles knock-out. Poor black rolled an anti-joker 2–1 and failed to get both checkers off. His only hope was that white rolled a 2–1 also (5.6 per cent chance). He didn't and white went through to the next round.

28 Under Biba Clock Rules the Director will place on each player's clock 12 seconds per move plus a reserve of two minutes for each point needed to complete a new match.

29 Crossovers are when you cross over from one quadrant to another.

30 *Backgammon Boot Camp* was written by Walter Trice.

glossary

accept a double	To agree to continue playing a game at twice the previous stakes. (*See* 'take' and 'double')
ace point	The first point in a player's home board – the 1-point.
ace point game	A position in a game in which a player has a checker(s) trapped on the opponent's ace-point and is waiting for a hit.
acey-deucey	A variation of backgammon in which the roll of 1 and 2 (or 2–1) gives the player extra turns, popularized in the US Navy.
action play	A specific type of play designed to provoke an exchange of hits, mainly used after an opponent has escaped his back checkers or runners.
active builder	A completely free checker that is able to make another point without being hit.
advanced anchor	An anchor on the opponent's four or five point.
air ball	An unexpectedly poor roll.
anchor	A point held by two or more of a player's checkers in an opponent's home board.
around the corner	A move from the opponent's outer board to the player's outer board.
attacking game	An attack on blots in a player's home board aimed at closing out an opponent. (*See* 'blitz')
automatic doubles	If both players roll the same number on the first roll of a game, the cube stakes are

to be doubled while the cube remains centred. This is an optional rule and is usually restricted to money games.

awkward number   A dice roll that causes the player's position to deteriorate.

back game   A position in which a player occupies two or more points in an opponent's home board. He then hopes to hit blots left by an opponent as the opponent brings checkers home and begins to bear them off. A successful backgammon depends heavily on timing. (*See* 'timing')

back checker   *See* 'runner'

backgammon   There are two meanings of backgammon:
- the game of backgammon
- a completed game of backgammon in which the losing player fails to bear off any checkers and still has one or more checkers on the bar or in the winner's home board. A backgammon is worth triple points.

backgammon server   A computer-based 'board' where backgammon players compete on a computer network set up by the server. Records, rankings and communications between players are also part of the services provided.

bar   The raised section (often the hinge) down the centre of a backgammon board dividing the home board from the outer board. Checkers are placed here after being hit. Checkers on the bar must re-enter before any other checkers can be moved.

bar-point   The 7-point, adjacent to the bar.

battle of primes   A type of position in which both players have trapped an opponent's checker or checkers behind a prime.

bear in   To bring a checker into your home board prior to bearing off.

bear off   The final stage of the game in which a player, having moved all his checkers into his home board, moves them off the board according to the dice roll.

beavers	In money play, an optional rule, agreed by both players prior to commencement of the game, in which when a player is doubled, he may immediately redouble (beaver) and still retain the doubling cube. As with a normal double/redouble the original doubler can accept or refuse the beaver.
bertha	To mistakenly play a 6–5 from the 24-point without noticing that your opponent has made his 6- and 7-points, thus blocking you in.
Biba	British Isles Backgammon Association.
big play	A bold aggressive play when a safer but less constructive play is available.
black	A colour used in backgammon articles referring to the darker of the two colours used.
blitz	an attack on blots in a player's home board aimed at closing out an opponent. (*See* also attacking game)
block	Points formed in front of an opponent's checkers to hinder their progress around the board.
blockade	Continuous blocks of points formed in order to prevent the escape of an opponent's runners.
blot	An exposed or lone checker on a point, being vulnerable to a hit.
blot-hitting contest	An exchange of rapid, often unprotected hits in which both players try to gain a key point.
board	There are several meanings: • the playing area of a backgammon game • one of the four segments that comprise the playing surface; home board or outer board • to 'make one's board' means to close out an opponent on the bar by closing all the points in your home board.
box	In a chouette, the player who plays against all the others.

break a point	Removing one of two of your checkers from a point you already occupy, thus leaving a blot.
break contact	A stage in the game where there is no longer any contact between opposing checkers.
break the board	Giving up established points in your home board.
break up	See 'break the board' and 'crunch'
builder	A spare checker used to make a point with others.
Calcutta auction	A lottery of entrants in a backgammon tournament. At the start of the tournament, players are auctioned off and the proceeds go into a pool to be distributed later to the buyers of the successful players. Sometimes players are grouped into fields, with each field sold as a package. The rules usually allow a player to buy back a portion of himself if he wants to increase his stake in the tournament.
candlesticks	A position where a player stacks many checkers on points he already occupies. Also known as 'stacking'.
captain	In a chouette, the leader of the team playing against the box.
cash	To offer a double when a player is certain his opponent will refuse to accept it.
centred cube	The starting position of the doubling cube in the centre of the bar prior to either player offering a double.
checker	See 'man'
chouette	A form of backgammon for more than two players where one player, known as the box, plays against a group of others who form a team led by a captain.
clean play	A move completed legally.
clear a point	See 'break a point'
close out	To 'make one's board', or to close out an opponent on the bar by closing all the points in your home board.
closed board	See 'close out'
closed point	A point containing two or more checkers.
cock shot	Re-entering off the bar with a 6–2 and

	hitting a blot on the 8-point when the only open point is the 2-point. (*See* 'joker')
cocked dice	An illegal roll of the dice. Both dice must come to rest flat (not cocked) on the playing surface to the right of the bar; otherwise they must be rolled again.
combination shot	Where both dice numbers are used together to form a roll greater than that of a single die.
come in	*See* 're-enter'
comeback shot	A roll that enables a checker on the bar to hit a blot.
communication	Keeping checkers within six pips of one another for mutual support.
consolidate	Tidy up one's checkers, reducing the number of blots, often prior to offering a double.
contact game	A position in which it is still possible for one player to hit or block the other. The opposite of 'break contact'.
count	*See* 'pip-count'
counter	*See* 'man'
cover a blot	To land a checker on one of your own, single, checkers thus making a point.
CPW(cubeless probability of winning)	A player's chances of winning the game if no doubling cube is being used.
Crawford rule	A stage in the game when the first player reaches match point. For this one game the cube cannot be used. In any subsequent games the cube can be used prior to any legal throw, except the opening roll. This game is known as the Crawford game named after John Crawford.
Crossover	Moving a checker from one segment to another, i.e. from outer board to home board, etc.
crunch	A position in which a player's prime falls apart due to the lack of alternative plays.
cube	*See* 'doubling cube'
cube decision	The choice of whether or not to offer a double, or the choice of whether to accept or refuse when a double has been offered.

cube equity	In money play with a doubling cube, the value of a position to one of the players compared with the current stake being played for. Cube equity considers cube ownership as it relates to the potential for future doubles, but does not consider the current value of the cube.
cube ownership	Players may only double when it is their turn to throw and must do so before throwing, but not after rolling cocked dice. If an opponent accepts the double they do so by placing the cube on their side of the board. Both players should ensure that the correct level is displayed.
dance	A dice roll that fails to re-enter a checker off the bar after having been hit.
dead cube	A cube that is of no redoubling value, i.e. the value when used would exceed the number of points an opponent would need to win the game.
dead checker	A checker deep in a player's home board; usually on the 1- and 2-points.
dead number	A die roll that cannot be played legally.
deep	*See* 'dead checker'
dice	Small cubes marked with dots 1 to 6 on each face, used to determine moves around the board. The plural of 'die'.
dice combination	The number of possible rolls (36) using two dice.
dice cup	A cup used to shake and roll the dice.
die	Singular of dice.
dilly builder	A builder that only lands on a point deep in your home board.
disengage	*See* 'break contact'
diversification	Spreading out the checkers in such a way as to increase the number of good rolls on a subsequent turn.
DMP	*See* 'double match point'
dominate	To be at least as good as in all respects. One play is said to dominate another (similar) play if it is as good as the other play by any measure of comparison. Spotting dominated plays can reduce the

	total number of plays to choose from in a given position.
double	An offer to play for twice the original stake.
double ducks	The roll of 2–2.
double game	*See* 'gammon'
double-hit	To hit two opponent's checkers in a single move.
double jeopardy	Potential for awkward rolls both next turn and the turn after.
double match point(DMP)	A match in which both players need just one more point to win; or a game in which the doubling cube has reached a level high enough that if either player wins the game they also win the match.
double out	To offer a double which, if accepted, will win the match for the doubler if he wins the game.
double roll	*See* 'roll a double'
double shot	A blot exposed to hits from two of an opponent's checkers.
doubles	Dice rolls with the same value, e.g. 6–6, 4–4 etc.
doubling cube	A cubical block with the numbers 2, 4, 8, 16, 32 and 64 marked on its faces, used for keeping track of the increase in stakes of a game and the player who has the right to make the next double.
doubling window	The range of winning percentages that may justify giving your opponent a cube that he should certainly take.
drop	To refuse to accept a double/redouble.
drop point	The maximum equity at which it is correct for a player to refuse a double.
dropper	A player on a backgammon server who avoids a loss by intentionally leaving a match before it is finished.
drop-take	Used in chouette, this is when some players in the team drop the double offered and others take.
duplication	A position in which two or more of the opponent's good moves both use the same number.
edge of a prime	An open point directly in front of an opponent's prime.

efficient double	An effective double when the recipient would be correct to either accept or refuse.
eject	To abandon an ace-point game to avoid losing a backgammon or gammon.
end game	The period at the end of the game when either player begins to bear off and there is no longer any contact.
enter	*See* 're-enter'
equity	The expected value of a backgammon position. Specifically, the sum of the values of the possible outcomes from a given position, with each value multiplied by its probability of occurrence.
expert backgammon	A computer program that plays backgammon and performs rollouts, written by Tom Weaver.
exposed checker	A blot within range of a direct shot.
extra cubes	An optional rule for chouettes used when only some of the players on the team accept a double from the box.
fan	A dice roll that fails to re-enter a checker off the bar. (*See* 'dance')
FIBS	The First Internet Backgammon Server; an electronic forum for playing backgammon with others from around the world, developed by Andreas Schneider.
FIBS rating	A number associated with each player based on that player's record of performance against other rated players. Every player starts with a rating of 1500.
fish	A poor backgammon money manager.
fly shot	An indirect shot using both dice with few combinations.
forced play	A roll of the dice for which there is only one legal play.
forward game	*See* 'running game'
free drop	In match play, after the Crawford game has been played and the trailing player has an even number of points to go, the option of the leading player to refuse a double without reducing the number of games the trailing player needs to win the match. (*See* also 'mandatory double')

free drop vigorish	In match play, after the Crawford game, the slight advantage the leader has when the trailer is two points away from victory because the leader has the option of refusing when the trailer offers a double.
freeze a builder	To leave a checker within reach of an opponent occupying a point with only two checkers, thus restricting their use as builders.
front a prime	Make the point immediately in front of an opponent's prime.
gammon	A completed game of backgammon in which the losing player has not borne off any checkers but doesn't have any on the bar or in their opponent's home board. A gammon is worth twice the current cube value.
gammon count	A method of assessing a player's chance of being gammoned.
gammon price	The relative value of winning a gammon versus winning a single game. Gammon price is computed as: $GP = (WG - W) \div (W - L)$ where: WG is the value of winning a gammon, W is the value of winning a single game, L is the value of losing a single game.
	In money play, the gammon price is 50 per cent. In match play, the gammon price depends on the score of the match and the level of the doubling cube; it can range anywhere from 0 (e.g. at double match point) to well over 100 per cent.
gammon rate	The fraction of games that end in a gammon or a backgammon. This includes games that would end in a gammon if they were played to completion but are not because a player doubles and the opponent refuses.
gammon vig (or gammon vigorish)	The additional equity resulting from the possibility of a gammon.
gap	Empty points or spaces between established points.
gin	A position in a game where it is impossible for one player to win no matter what rolls he gets.

go out	To achieve the points necessary to win a match.
golden point	Your opponent's 5-point.
guff (or guffy)	A player's 1-point. (*See* 'ace-point')
GWC	Game-winning chances.
half a roll	One number showing on a pair of tossed dice.
Hari-Kiri play	A play that exposes blots for the purpose of recirculating the player's checkers.
heavy point	A point with more than three checkers on it.
hit	To land on a point where there is an opponent's lone checker (blot), thus putting him on the bar.
hit and cover	To hit (as in hit above) and then continue to cover your own blot, in a single play with a single checker.
hit and pass	*See* 'pick and pass'
hit and split	To move a back checker and hit an opponent's blot elsewhere on the board in one move.
hit loose	To hit an opposing checker at a time when the player's own blots are in danger of a return hit.
holding game	A game in which one player occupies a point or points on the opponent's side of the board to make it more difficult for the opponent to bring home his checkers safely.
Holland rule	An optional rule for match play to be used in conjunction with the Crawford rule. It states that after the Crawford game neither player may double until two rolls have been played by each side. Named after Tim Holland.
home board	Points 1 to 6; the segment of the playing surface where players bear off their checkers.
inactive builder	A checker that is currently part of a block or prime that might be used later to form other blocks.
indirect shot	*See* 'combination shot'
inner table	*See* 'home board'
Jacoby rule	A rule, mostly used in money play, that disallows gammons and backgammons

unless either player has accepted a double during the game. Attributed to Oswald Jacoby.

Janowski's formula A formula devised by Englishman Rick Janowski for estimating match equity at a given match score. It says that the probability of the leading player winning the match is: $0.5 + 0.85d \div (t+6)$ where d is the difference in match score and t is the number of points the trailing player has to go. (*See* 'Neil's numbers')

Jellyfish A neural net computer program that plays backgammon, analyses and performs roll-outs.

jeopardy Potential for awkward rolls on a future turn.

joker An exceptionally good roll, especially a roll that reverses the likely outcome of the game. An example of a joker would be a roll of double 6s to bear off your last four checkers when your opponent otherwise wins on his next turn. (*See* 'cock shot')

Kauder paradox The fact that in money play with the Jacoby rule in effect, a position can theoretically be both a proper double and a proper beaver. By doubling, the underdog gets full value for his potential gammons, thus raising his equity. However, as long as this equity remains negative, the doubler's opponent should naturally beaver.

kibitzer A spectator who often offers unwanted advice or comment.

kill a checker To move an extra checker deep within a player's home board where it serves no useful purpose. (*See* 'dead checker')

kill a number To create a position in which a specific die value cannot be played on the next turn.

last roll position The last position of a game in which both players still have a chance to win.

leave a shot To leave a blot exposed within range of an opponent's checkers.

loose checker *See* 'blot'

lover's leap An opening roll of 6–5 played from the 24-point to the 13-point.

make a point	To place two or more checkers on a point. (*See* 'anchor')
man	One of the 30 counters that are moved around the board according to rolls of the dice. Each player has 15 men (checkers) in opposing colours, e.g. black and white. (Also known as piece, checker or stone.)
mandatory double	A situation possible in match play in which it is correct for a player to double based solely on the match score. In any post-Crawford rule game, it is correct for the trailing player to double at the earliest opportunity because the loss of the game, doubled or not, also means the loss of the match. (See also 'free drop')
mandatory extras	An optional rule for money play which says that whenever a double is offered and accepted, the doubler has the right to give his opponent an extra cube at the same level. The extra cube must be accompanied by a payment equal to one half of its value. The receiver then has two cubes that he may use together or separately for making future doubles.
market gainer	Any sequence of two rolls (one by a player and one by his opponent) that leads to a position where the opponent would be willing to accept if he were offered a double. Knowing the number of market gainers can help a player decide whether he should double or play on for a gammon.
market loser	Any sequence of two rolls (one by a player and one by his opponent) that leads to a position in which the opponent is no longer willing to accept if he is offered a double. (Also known as a market-losing sequence.) Knowing the number of market losers can help a player decide whether he should double now or wait.
match	A series of games between two players that ends when one player wins by accumulating the required number of points. (*See* 'match play')

match equity	A player's expectation of winning a match at a given match score. The value of a position in the context of the current match score.
match equity table	A table showing a player's expectation of winning a match from various match scores.
match play	The competition system used in tournaments in which two participants play a series of games that ends when one player accumulates a required number of points. Each game is worth one, two, or three points (for a single game, gammon or backgammon) multiplied by the value of the doubling cube.
match point	A time in the match when the leading player needs just one more point to win.
mid-point	Your 13-point; the opponent's 12-point.
middle game	A stage in the game after the opening moves and before the bear off.
mixed roll	Two thrown dice with different numbers on their upper face.
modern game	A style of play popularized in the 1970s that emphasizes slotting, making advanced anchors and playing back games.
money play	The normal style of competition in which games are played independently and the competitors bet on the result. For each game, the loser pays the winner the agreed initial stake multiplied by the value of the doubling cube and further multiplied by two for a gammon or three for a backgammon.
move	The advancement of a player's checker according to the value showing on one of the dice he rolls. There are three types of legal moves. A player may:

- **enter a checker from the bar** When a player has a checker on the bar, this is his only legal move
- move a checker the number of pips indicated on the die to a lower open point, possibly hitting an opposing blot

• bear off a checker, if all of the player's checkers are in his home board.

mutual holding game	A game in which both players occupy a point or points on the opponent's side of the board to make it more difficult for the other player to bring home his checkers safely.
MWC	match-winning chances.
Neil's numbers	A mnemonic device invented by Neil Kazaross for estimating match equity based on the current match score. It says that the leader's percentage probability of winning the match is 50 + his lead multiplied by the Neil's numbers.

Points trailer needs	3	4	5	6	7	8	9	10	11	12	13	14	15
Neil's Numbers	10	9	8	7		6			5				

(See 'Janowski's formula')

no-brainer	A stage of the game after which there is no further contact between opposing sides and the dice, rather than better playing, will dictate who wins.
no contact	*See* 'break contact'
normalized match score	A match score expressed in terms of the number of points each player still needs to win the match, as opposed to the number of points they have won so far.
nullo play	A play that cannot be profitable for any possible sequence of future rolls.
on roll	The player whose turn it is now is 'on roll'.
on the bar	A blot that has been hit and is waiting to re-enter. (*See* 'bar')
one-point game	See 'ace-point game'
open point	Any empty point on the board not occupied by two or more checkers.
opening roll	The first roll of a game, in which both players each throw one die and the higher roller takes both as the first move.
otter	An immediate redouble (while retaining ownership of the cube) by the player who just accepted a raccoon.

outer board	Points 7 to 12; the segment of the playing surface where the dice are rolled. (*See* 'inner table')
outer table	*See* 'outer board'
outfield	The outer board, particularly points nine, ten, and eleven.
outside prime	A series of blocked points of which the majority are in the outer board.
own the cube	The player who last accepted a double and the only one allowed to redouble.
pass	To refuse a double.
pick-and-pass	To hit an opponent's blots and then continue to land on one of your own points.
pip	A dot on a die. Also the distance between points expressed as a unit, e.g. the distance from the 24-point to the 13-point (mid-point) is 11 pips.
pip-count	The total number of points (or pips) that a player must move his checkers to bring them home and bear them off.
play	The movement of checkers in accordance with the dice roll.
point	One of the 24 narrow triangles, 12 on each side of a backgammon board, where the players' checkers sit. The points are numbered, for each player, 1 to 12 across the near side of the board and 13 to 24 in the other direction across the far side of the board. Either player's 1-point is the other player's 24-point.
point on a blot	Hitting an opponent's blot with two checkers at once.
PRaT	position, race and threat; a means of assessing doubling windows.
pressure	To directly threaten an opponent's builder or blot, forcing them to move it, make the point or be hit.
prime	Two or more consecutive blocks, which restrict an opponent's checkers. Ideally primes should be 4-, 5- or 6-blocks.
prop (or proposition)	A prearranged position played several times, usually for money, as a means of

settling a dispute over which checker play or cube action is best.

pure play
: Playing in such a way as to make a prime using builders and slotting.

pure race
: *See* 'break contact'

quadrant
: One quarter of the playing area on a backgammon board.

raccoon
: An immediate redouble by the player who just accepted a beaver.

race
: A stage in the game where there is no longer any contact between opposing checkers and both players are racing to the finish.

rail
: *See* 'bar'

recirculate
: To purposely leave blots to be hit and thus to re-enter the game to gain timing and to preserve points.

recube vig (or recube vigorish)
: The value of cube ownership to the player being offered a double.

redouble
: A second or subsequent turn of the doubling cube.

re-enter
: To move a checker from the bar to a point in an opponent's home board according to the dice roll.

reference position
: A position of known value used as a guide in assessing the value of similar positions.

refuse a double
: To resign a game at the current stakes rather than continue to play at twice the stakes, after the opponent offers a double.

return shot
: A hit an opponent will have on his next roll after being hit.

roll a double
: When both dice fall on the same number. In backgammon this double roll is moved four times instead of the normal two for non-double rolls.

roll out
: To analyse a position by repeatedly playing it to a later point in the game using different dice rolls. To estimate the equity of a position by playing to completion the same position many times using different random dice rolls and averaging the results (often using a

computer). Such an estimate is called a roll out.

rolling prime	A prime that is moved forward by using checkers from the rear.
root number	A particular roll of the dice that causes a position to crunch.
run	To move your last checker from an opponent's home board.
runner	The farthest checker from home; usually in an opponent's home board or on the bar.
running game	A stage in the game where there is no longer any contact between opposing checkers and both players are racing to the finish. (*See* 'race')
safe	A play after which you are not in danger of being hit.
safety a checker	To move a checker out of danger. (*See* 'safe')
safety play	A play that in the long run is not the strongest or most constructive play available but instead leaves an opponent with the least possible good moves on his next roll.
save a gammon	To avoid losing two points (a gammon) by bearing off at least one checker.
save a number	To play in such a way as to ensure that certain dice rolls are not forced and can be moved elsewhere.
semi-active builder	A checker which may or may not be available to make another point, depending on the roll.
settlement	A payment of points by one player to the other based on the fair value of a position. (*See* 'equity')
settlement equity	The value of a position in a money game to one of the players and the fair value, as a factor of the initial stake, that should change hands in lieu of finishing the game. Settlement equity is equal to cube equity times the current value of the doubling cube.
shift points	To move from one point to make another one. Often done to make a better point or to avoid leaving blots.

shot	A chance to hit an opponent's blot. Direct shots hit using a single die. Indirect shots hit using both dice for one checker.
shut out	*See* 'close out'
single game	A completed game that is not a gammon or backgammon – either a game in which the losing player has borne off at least one checker or a game that ends when a double is refused.
single shot	A blot exposed to hits from one of an opponent's checkers.
slot	To play a single checker on to an empty point with the intention of covering it next turn.
slot and split	To play a checker into an open point in your home board and move a back checker. (*See* 'splot')
Snowie	Neural network backgammon program. Available from Biba.
spare checker	An extra checker on a point that can be used for hitting or making a point without leaving behind a blot.
split	To separate two checkers that are together on a point (typically the 24-point) and leave them as blots.
splot	A combination of 'split' and 'slot' coined by Chuck Bowers. For example, with a 4–1 roll; 4 is played 24/23 (split) and the 1 is played 6/5 (slot). (*See* 'split' and 'slot')
squeeze	To take advantage of the opponent's compulsion to move any playable roll.
stacking	*See* 'candlesticks'
Staine's rule	An optional rule regarding doubles wherein all doubles rolled are classed as non-doubles and can only be moved twice instead of the usual four times. (*See* 'roll a double')
stake	The amount wagered by the participants in a game of backgammon. The current stake is the initial stake multiplied by the value of the doubling cube.
stay back	To remain in an opponent's home board.
steam	To lose control and take risks or play recklessly. Usually preceded by a run of 'bad

luck' after which the player is convinced that the dice are against him and he plays progressively worse!

stretched	A position barren of spare checkers or builders and thus prone to awkward numbers.
strip a point	To leave just two checkers on a point that previously had more.
stripped	A position barren of spare checkers or builders and thus prone to awkward numbers.
switch points	To give up one point to make another in the same move.
sydney	The roll of 1 and 6 to escape a prime, usually from the bar and often hitting a blot.
tailgate	To roll prematurely, i.e. before your opponent has picked up their dice.
take	To accept a double.
take/drop decision	The choice of whether to accept or refuse a double.
TD-gammon	A computer program that plays backgammon, written by Gerald Tesauro.
tempo	A unit of time in positional development equal to half a roll.
tempo move	A hit designed to forestall the opponent by depriving him of half a roll when he threatens to hit a blot or make an important point.
Thorp count	A formula devised by Edward O. Thorp for making doubling decisions in pure race games. It is a modification of the basic pip-count that takes into account some elements of checker distribution. Each player's Thorp count is his pip-count, plus two for each of his checkers still on the board, minus one for each of his occupied home-board points, plus one for each checker on his one point. Then the player on roll increases his count by 10 per cent if it is more than 30. Thorp advises: Double any time your count does not exceed your opponent's by more than two. Redouble any time

your count does not exceed your opponent's by more than one. Accept if your count does not exceed the doubler's by more than two.

timing The general rate of advancement of a player's and his opponent's checkers viewed in terms of their likely position at a future crucial point in the game, partially controllable by the leaving of blots to be hit and the hitting or not hitting of adverse blots.

too good to double A position in which a player should not double even though the opponent has a clear drop, because the player has a higher equity by playing on for a gammon.

trap play A deliberate attempt to force an opponent off his anchor, thereby exposing blots and possible gammons.

tric-trac French (among others) for backgammon.

triple game *See* 'backgammon'

triple shot A blot exposed to hits from three of an opponent's checkers.

turn The sequence of actions that each player takes in alternation that consists of possibly offering a double, rolling the dice, playing the roll and picking up the dice.

turn the cube Offering a double.

under the gun A blot in the opponent's home board when it is within direct range of three or more of the opponent's builders and therefore in danger of being pointed on.

vig (or vigorish) The small additional considerations that affect the total equity of a position, such as gammon vigorish and recube vigorish.

volatility The changeability of the equity of a position. A position of high volatility is one that is likely to see a large change in equity as a result of the player's or the opponent's next roll. A position's volatility is a consideration for a player deciding whether or not to offer a double.

wash A blitzing technique that involves breaking a higher home-board point in order to hit a blot on a lower home-board point.

wastage	The expected loss in pips from dice rolls that are not fully used during bear off.
weaver	A deliberate misplay in the hope that an inferior opponent will take his offered cube next turn.
white	A colour used in backgammon articles referring to the lighter of the two colours used.

index